# Why Israel Is Supernatural

## The EAGLE, the LION, & MIRACLES

## Rabbi MICHAEL ZEITLER
## and Rabbi GAIL ZEITLER

BRONZE BOW PUBLISHING

Unless otherwise indicated, Scriptures are taken from the BIBLE: NEW INTERNATIONAL VERSION®.
Copyright © 1973, 1978, 1984 by International Bible Society. Used by permission of Zondervan Publishing
House. All rights reserved.

Scriptures noted KJV are taken from the *King James Version* of the Bible.

Scriptures noted NASB are taken from the *New American Standard Bible®*. Copyright © 1960, 1962, 1963,
1968, 1971, 1972, 1973, 1975, 1977, 1995 by the Lockman Foundation. Used by permission.

Scriptures noted CJB are taken from the *Complete Jewish Bible*. Copyright © 1998. Used by permission of
the Messianic Jewish Resources International.

Words and music to "Jews and Gentiles" by Joel Chernoff © 1999 Galilee of the Nations Music/ASCAP
Admin. By Fricout Music Co. /ASCAP.

ISBN 13: 978-1-932458-76-3; ISBN 10: 1-932458-76-X

Published by Bronze Bow Publishing, Inc.
2600 E. 26th Street, Minneapolis, MN 55406

You can reach us on the Internet at www.bronzebowpublishing.com.

Literary development and cover/interior design by Koechel Peterson & Associates, Inc., Minneapolis,
Minnesota.

Printed in the United States of America

# Dedication

First and foremost, to the Lord Yeshua,
who's anointing is upon this book.

To my loving deceased wife, Gail,
without whom this book never would have been written.
She basically took a sermon I had taught in a very high level
Christian financial conference to millionaires
and turned it into the book you are now reading.
A copy of the DVD on this message was put
into the hands of the then President George W. Bush.

To my sister, Bobbie,
and to my brother, Dick.

To Gail's daughter, Jessica,
who encouraged her and knew
her mom would get it done.

To my son, Jeremy,
for his curiosity in everything she said,
and my daughter, Elisha,
who encouraged me in ways
she couldn't have ever imagined.

# About the Author

Rabbis Michael and Gail Zeitler were the founders of Baruch Ha Shem Messianic Ministries International. Rabbi Michael speaks at churches and conferences around the world, encouraging the body of Messiah to embrace what was stolen from them—their Jewish roots. Michael and Gail were ordained by Messianic Vision through Sid Roth. They had previously founded and led two Messianic congregations in upstate New York. They produced a TV show called *Celebrate the Messiah* and were guests on TBN's *Praise the Lord* several times. Michael completed *Why Israel Is Supernatural*, originally his wife's project, after she passed away in 2007.

# Acknowledgments

I want to thank Pastor Don Moore, my spiritual father, mentor, and friend, without whose encouragement and belief in me this book would have never been completed.

To Sid Roth, my mentor and friend, who knew my limitations but pushed beyond even when I did not think I could go any farther.

To my spiritual dad, Pastor Don Leslie, who through it all was there and supported me all along the way.

For all my friends and spiritual family, including Rich, Kathie, and Grace Ienuso, Michael Flaherty, and Phil and Paige Todd, who kept me going even when I wanted to give up after losing my Gail.

And most of all, for the Lord Yeshua, whom Gail and I love so much, who gave us this message for the Last Days to be heard so all would know the truth. Thank you!

# Table of Contents

*If you are wrong in your understanding of Israel, you will be open for End-Time deceptions in many other areas. This book settles all misunderstandings about God's position on Israel.*

Sid Roth, Host of *It's Supernatural*

*Knowing the heart of Israel and America and the prophetic connections is surely an area of expertise that Rabbi Michael Zeitler can expound upon. New insights and deeper understanding spring forth from him to help others grasp this big topic.*

Pastor Don Moore, Living Word Chapel

*A masterpiece on God's plan and purposes for Israel. Truly, there are no coincidences, only God-incidences in Supernatural Israel!*

Pastor/Teacher Rich Ienuso, Lighthouse Ministries

# Introduction

Have you ever wondered about God's plan for the United States and Israel? This book contains insights and revelations to the relationship between Israel and the U.S. all the way back to the beginning. Find out what our presidents were thinking about this Jewish nation, and their attitudes concerning the same. This book is for Jew and Gentile alike to discover the real stories, the real facts behind all the politics and lies. Find out about the true heroes and how they risked everything to bring the truth to reality.

We will also trace the history of the ebb and flow of the birthing of this tiny and mighty nation of Israel. Only God could produce the results that are stated in Isaiah 66:8, *"Can a country be born in a day or a nation be brought forth in a moment?"* Read in-depth as we reveal the true miracles behind the scenes that have taken place in every war Israel was involved with. You will be amazed at the hand of God through the decades!

As we are moving toward the End Times, it is time for all to be revealed—where Israel fits into the scheme of our world events. This book will present those answers and show how it has been transpiring. Learn about the lies and deception that have been surrounding Israel's place in the world, and discover how God is bringing the truth to the light through divine providence. Israel and Jerusalem are "the apple" of God's eye, and no one on this earth will ever change that fact.

Everyone needs to be informed and understand so they can prepare for the future, and this book will show you how!

# 1

# *Why Is Israel* Supernatural?

God's hand has been upon the Promised Land since time immemorial, and He covets it with great love. Over the ages, we see time and time again how He loves His land and protects it. He chose Abraham and his future generations to make a covenant with the land, because His Son, the Messiah, would eventually emanate from that race of people. He could have chosen any race, but He chose the Jewish people.

Even when the land was abandoned because of the disobedience of the people, He still kept it and covered it with His hand. He decided before the beginning of the foundations of the earth that this was where the New Jerusalem would reside in the future. We see in the Scriptures repeatedly that this land is a portal for heaven, with angels ascending and descending. Nowhere else is this more prevalent than in the land God holds so dear, "the apple of His eye."

As we trace history, we see the incredulity of a land that continues to survive in spite of all the conquerors and their devastation. Why is God so interested in this tiny nation that is smaller than the state of Delaware? Because it is where His heart is—where He chose to place His very presence in a structure made by the hands of men. This is where His Son was born into the world as a baby to become a man to redeem the world. This is where Satan will try but fail to bring defeat to the ultimate future of Israel.

Story after story recounts all that God has done with this land, and how the enemy has never succeeded in destroying it. There is no more commonplace on the face of the earth to see miracles, signs, and wonders. Despite battles and destruction, plagues, famines, and disasters, it continues to remain fortified in God's everlasting grip. It plays into God's plan for the dramatic End-Time events that will take place in the future. Nothing can stop the plan of God for Israel, for He will miraculously accomplish it all.

The war described in Ezekiel 38–39 shows the world just how supernatural Israel is. As the world watches the armies coming from the north to attack this tiny land, God lifts His hand and vanquishes His love's enemies. In one fell swoop, they are all destroyed, and all the glory goes to God. It is His supernatural land, and no weapon formed against it shall prosper.

Throughout history, God has intervened over and over for His land and people. Although outnumbered greatly by their enemies, Israel's mighty Joshua always triumphed, despite the overwhelming odds. Remember the battle when the sun and moon stood in their place (Joshua 10)? These types of battles took place only in the covenant land of Israel, and its borders were greatly expanded. Remember how Gideon was outnumbered and never had to fight his enemy (Judges 7). King Hezekiah was instructed by God's servant Isaiah on what specifically to do in every battle (2 Kings 19). King David was directed by the prophets and always succeeded in battle, as the Lord would go before him and defeat the armies.

Even in the recent wars that have taken place in Israel, the righteous hand of God has supernaturally circumvented defeats and setbacks. There have been so many documented accounts of impossible odds to overcome, and yet every time God turned it around. In Chapter 9, "Miracles—Old and New," those accountings are fully reported.

Many people, both Jewish and Gentile, have testified to the fact that something about the land of Israel is different than anywhere else on the planet. They have seen the manifest hand of God in His land to prevent disasters from taking place. Since His land was raised from the dead in 1948, people from all nations have seen miracles unfold before their eyes—things that cannot be explained except by the hand of God truly intervening in situations. Some may claim this has happened in many other places, but in His land it is with great frequency. He has prospered His land with beauty and fruit and produce coming from an arid desert environment, by breathing His life into it. Someone once said if you live in Israel, you have to believe in miracles.

Where is more world news reported than in this little nation of Israel? The book of Ezekiel states that in the Last Days Jerusalem will become a stumbling stone to the nations. This scripture is being fulfilled right before our eyes.

God wants all the focus to be on "the apple of His eye," and He watches carefully how she is treated. The quartet of nations (United States, European Union, United Nations, and Russia) tries to control this land that God holds so precious in His sight. They will not prevail, however, because this supernatural land does not belong to them. In Chapter 13, "The Peace Process and Natural Disasters," you will see the justice of God as He expresses His displeasure when someone tries to blacken the apple of His eye. We must realize that it is the truth, whether we believe or not. Only the facts matter, and that is why Israel is supernatural.

God's hand will always remain on this precious land, and nothing will ever change that. Those who bless Israel will be blessed, and those who curse Israel will be cursed.

# 2

# *A History of* America and Israel

Christopher Columbus (1451–1506) was the Italian navigator and explorer whose voyages across the Atlantic Ocean ushered in the first period of sustained contact between Europe and the New World of the Americas. Columbus was a devout Catholic who felt predestined, chosen for a mission. He felt his name, Christopher, which means "Christ-bearer," was evidence of his destiny. He searched the Scriptures and thought he found assurance for a call to sail to the far reaches of the globe with the Christian message. Zechariah 9:10 said that "He will proclaim peace to the nations. His rule will extend from sea to sea and from the River to the ends of the earth." Based on the Bible, he believed that the earth was round instead of flat, making it a shorter trip to Asia traveling west by sea than going east by land.[1]

Controversy surrounds Columbus's background and motivation. Was he a Jewish *converso*, one who had accepted Christianity? Was he a greedy merchant or a holy man on a mission? Was he looking for spices or for a Jewish homeland? As the Inquisition (a tribunal established in 1476 by Catholic monarchs Ferdinand II of Aragon and Isabella I of Castile intended to enforce Catholic orthodoxy in their kingdoms) raged in Spain, many Jews became Christians or hid their Jewish identity in order to save their lives and their families.

The first biographer to claim that Columbus was Jewish was author Salvador de Madariaga in 1949. The author pointed out that Columbus's name in Spanish, *Colon*, was a Jewish name. Columbus associated with many Jewish "New Christians." No one knows for sure, but it seems likely that Columbus was a Messianic Jew from all his references to the Old Testament prophets.[2]

The Jews in Spain suffered unthinkably during the Inquisition. They were forced to both accept Catholicism and declare faith in Christ or be tortured and killed. The ones who became sincere believers were the *conversos*, or converted ones; *marranos* were those who pretended to be Christians but secretly practiced Judaism. *Marrano* was a derisive term meaning "pig," a non-kosher animal.

The Vatican ordered the Inquisition to inquire as to whether each *converso* was sincere. Before too long, the Inquisitors were killing every Jew they caught, whether a *marrano* or not.

If Columbus did have Jewish ancestry, he would have gone to great lengths to hide it from the king and queen of Spain! He would have been a *converso*, a sincere convert, with a Jewish background that caused him to want to find a Jewish homeland.[3]

Jewish or not, it is clear that Columbus could not have made his voyage without the help of prominent New Christians. He plotted his course with the aid of three Jewish scientists who had discovered new theories and equipment to judge distance and direction from the stars. Jewish financiers provided the bulk of the funds necessary for the trip. *Converso* members of the Spanish court interceded for him, convincing Queen Isabella to approve of the venture and provide some of the funding.

It is a myth that Queen Isabella sold her jewels to finance Columbus's trip. The Jewish-American Hall of Fame invites us to "learn that it was Spanish Jewry, not Spanish jewelry that paid for Columbus's voyage of discovery."

Why would these high-ranking and wealthy *conversos* help Columbus find Asia? Coinciding with Columbus's journey was the expulsion of all Jews from Spain. Columbus's three ships set sail on August 3, 1492, the very same day as the deadline for the expulsion. It was the saddest date on the Jewish calendar, *Tisha B'Av*. On that day, the Second Temple had been destroyed by the Romans in A.D. 70, scattering the people of Judea and commencing the Jewish exile from the Holy Land. Many other tragedies occurred on *Tisha B'Av* throughout the centuries.

Might Columbus, the *conversos* who helped him, and his crew, which included at least five Jews, have been motivated by the need to find a place for the Spanish Jews to go? Could they have been planning to use the spices and gold of Asia to buy back Palestine from the Turks?

Columbus was fascinated by the Old Testament prophets and by the End Times. He quoted many prophetic scriptures in his *Book of Prophecies*, proving that he believed he was fulfilling many of those prophecies. Describing his motive, Columbus stated: "Who can doubt that this fire was not merely mine, but also the Holy Spirit who encouraged me with a radiance of marvelous illumination from his sacred Scriptures,...urging me to press forward?" He felt that Almighty God had directly brought about his journey: "With a hand that could be felt, the Lord opened my mind to the fact that it would be possible...and He opened my will to desire to accomplish that project.... The Lord purposed that there should be something miraculous in this matter of the voyage to the Indies."

As we now know, Columbus did not reach Asia but discovered two continents unknown except by ancient Norse Vikings and the native's inhabitants. Columbus's faith in God set the stage for many immigrants who came later, the early colonists.

## EARLY COLONISTS

From Plymouth Rock to today, passion for God helped form this country, but most of us have been taught incorrectly about the first colonists. Their faith in God is ignored in the revisionist textbooks in our schools. We call the immigrants to the New World "Pilgrims," but they called themselves "Comers." They came here to start a new world with God as their ruler. The settlers who sailed in the *Mayflower* were the First Comers. When they stepped ashore in 1620, William Bradford's words at Plymouth Rock were, "Come, let us declare the word of God in Zion."[4]

So who were these people?

The Church of England was aligned with the Catholic Church until King Henry VII (1491–1547) took it over, but he retained all the Catholic trappings. The king merely replaced the pope with himself as far as England was concerned. During the great part of his reign, he brutally suppressed the influence of the Protestant Reformation in England.

As the Reformation reached England, the Puritans sought to purify and reform the Church. Most Puritans worked within the Church, but some, the Separatists, gave up and started their own churches.[5]

The First Comers to America were Separatists. They were members of the All Saints' Parish Church in England. King Henry had decreed that it was illegal to miss a Church of England Sunday service or to hold any other services. Two Separatist pastors who did were executed![6] Translating the Bible into English was also taboo.

So the entire All Saints' Parish Church moved to Amsterdam to escape the Church of England. From a remote point on the shore, they sailed out of England by cover of darkness. Some were caught and detained for a month. From Amsterdam, they all moved to Leiden, another city in Holland, trying to find employment.[7]

The members of the All Saints' Church decided to leave Holland to protect their congregation from assimilating into Dutch culture; besides, they found that the struggle to learn the Dutch language and find jobs became too much to bear. In the New World, they hoped to prosper and draw new church members from England.

This church of Separatists also heard about armies approaching Leiden. The Eighty Years' War was the first struggle to overthrow the rule of Philip II of Spain, the overlord of the Hapsburg Netherlands.

As the Netherlands won its independence from Spain, it became more and more dangerous for All Saints' to conduct religious activities.

The congregation sailed across the Atlantic together. They planned to settle along the Hudson River in New York, but the wind blew them off course to the future Massachusetts, at Plymouth Rock. Some other Comers who came later were the Quakers to Pennsylvania and the French Huguenots to upstate New York, South Carolina, and southern Virginia.

Most early settlements in America were not religious but were either business ventures, groups of people escaping economic or political hardships, or wealthy landholders trying to establish feudal fiefdoms, taking along indentured servants for free labor.

Who were Pilgrims and who were Puritans? A pilgrim is anyone who goes on a religious journey; therefore, "pilgrim" does describe all the Comers. The Puritans were all those who sought to purify the Church of England, either within it or without. The First Comers on the *Mayflower* were Puritans who separated themselves from the Church of England. The settlers of the later and much larger Massachusetts Bay Colony were Pilgrims and Puritans, but not Separatists. From their colony at Boston, they maintained their affiliation with the Church of England.

For both groups, the Bible was the final authority.

Back in Europe, the Comers had suffered persecution, torture, and murder as either the Church of England or the Catholic Church tried to force them to renounce their beliefs and submit to either King Henry or to the pope. They suffered much the same as the Jews did during the Inquisition. It is no wonder the settlers thought of themselves as New Jews, relating their voyage to the story of Exodus. They made their exodus across the Atlantic to the New World. They thought of these shores as the New Jerusalem. They even named their children Old Testament names, such as David and Sarah, and called their towns Salem and Providence.

They all were Restorationists, later known as Christian Zionists. Zionism is an international nationalist political movement that, in its broadest sense, calls for the existence of a sovereign Jewish national homeland. Zionism is based on historical ties and religious traditions linking the Jewish people to the land of Israel.

How many of us are aware that the earliest Americans longed for God to restore Israel? The new comers were fascinated with eschatology, the study of the End Times, or the Last Days.[8] Interest in the End Times led to interest in God's promises to His chosen people to return them to the land of Israel, although at the time the thought of Israel restored was as remote as the moon!

Their motivation was not so much love of any individual Jewish person, but their desire to see Jesus Christ return in the Second Coming. The book of Revelation and the Major and Minor Prophets revealed that Jesus would not return until Israel was restored.

Ironically, until the pogroms (a form of riot directed against a particular group, whether ethnic, religious, or other, and characterized by killings and destruction of their homes, businesses, and religious centers) against the Jews and even until the Holocaust, Christians were more anxious to see the Jews return to Israel than the Jews were. Jewish people were generally thriving in the countries they lived in (except Spain and Portugal). They had no desire to go to the vast wasteland that Palestine had become, especially under the control of the Turks.

The famous Thanksgiving dinner that the Pilgrims shared with the natives was actually a Feast of Tabernacles, or *Succoth*, that was held on October 6, 1621—not in November. The Pilgrims celebrated all the Feasts of Israel!

# IN THE 1700s

The Founding Fathers of the U.S. followed the Bible. As the new nation grew, every president spoke from his heart about restoring the Jews to their homeland.

Between the American Revolutionary War (1775–1783) and the signing of the Constitution (1787), the U.S. had no strong central government. The states were joined in a loose alliance called the Continental Congress. Once the Articles of Confederation were ratified in 1781, the president of the Continental Congress was recognized as the leader of the new nation.

The first president of the U.S. in Congress Assembled was John

Hanson. Some scholars claim that he was actually our first president, while others say that his leadership was unimportant, but in 1781 he was the man in charge!

John Boudinot was the second president. In 1783, he signed the Treaty of Paris for the U.S., ending the Revolutionary War with Britain.

The Constitution was crafted and ratified on September 17, 1787, giving greater power to the federal government. It called for the president to be the commander-in-chief of the armed forces. George Washington was the first president of the U.S. under the Constitution.

Boudinot believed that the Native Americans were the lost tribes of Israel and wrote a book about it: *Star in the West, or, a Humble Attempt to Discover the Long Lost Ten Tribes of Israel: Preparatory to Their Return to Their Beloved City, Jerusalem.*

In 1783, the state of Pennsylvania required all assemblymen to declare their belief in the Old and the New Testament. Jewish leaders protested, since that would exclude Jews from public office. Although their petition failed in their state, their wishes were honored by the draftees of the U.S. Constitution, which does not include such a religious oath.

During his 1790 visit to Newport, Rhode Island, George Washington reassured the Jewish community that the equality he fought for included the Jews. In a reply to a letter sent by the leader of Newport Jewish community, Washington said, "For happily the Government of the United States, which gives to bigotry no sanction, to persecution no assistance, requires only that they who live under its protection, should demean themselves as good citizens. May the Children of the Stock of Abraham, who dwell in this land, continue to merit and enjoy the good will of the other Inhabitants; while every one shall sit under his own vine and fig tree, and there shall be none to make him afraid."[9]

## IN THE 1800s

No discussion of early America's attitude toward Israel would be complete without introducing Mordecai Manuel Noah, "The First American Jew," the first Jew born in the U.S. to reach national prominence. Noah's name seems to have been lost from American history books, but not the books in Israel, where he is considered a hero. During his lifetime (1785–1841), he was the best-known Jew in America.

Many of the early presidents' comments about Israel and the Jews were in response to Noah's speeches and letters. Sixty years before Zionism began among the Jews in Europe, and more than a 100 years before Israel became a nation, Mordecai Noah campaigned for a Jewish homeland.

Noah descended from Portuguese Jews. His father not only served in the American Revolution, but helped to fund the war. While living in New York City, Noah founded several newspapers, which he used as tools for his political opinions. His powerful articles urged the U.S. to fight the British in the War of 1812. Noah also became the most well-known American playwright of the early 1800s, as well as a top figure in New York City politics. If that wasn't enough, he was a leader and spokesman for the Jewish community in America.

In 1811, Noah was appointed as the consul (ambassador) to Tunisia under President James Madison. As consul, he won the freedom of a group of kidnapped Americans who had been shanghaied from the Massachusetts coast by Algerian pirates and held in Tunis as slaves. What an interesting switch for a descendant of Hebrew slaves in Egypt!

However, Noah was fired by Madison's Secretary of State, James Monroe. Monroe's letter gave the reason for his dismissal: "At the time of your appointment, as Consul to Tunis, it was not known that the religion which you profess would form an obstacle to the exercise of your Consular functions."[10] Noah, along with many others, cried, "Outrage! Bigotry!"

The writer of that dismissal letter would become the next president.

Noah turned his attention to the plight of Jews worldwide. He worked zealously toward gathering them into a safe place. He spoke to Americans about what great citizens the Jews would be. He spoke to Jews in Europe and Asia about how great living in America would be.

At first, Noah attempted to create a homeland in America. In 1825, he established a Jewish colony in Grand Island, New York, near Niagara

Falls. He called it Ararat, after the mountain in Turkey where Noah's ark landed. That effort failed; no one came to live there.

After that, Noah became convinced that the only hope for the Jewish people was to regain Palestine. He gave speeches and wrote letters to three successive presidents to convince them to use America's power and wealth to buy back or capture the Promised Land from the Turks. His famous speech, "Discourse on the Restoration of the Jews," reminded Christians that it was their Christian duty to do all they could to restore Israel to the Jews.

## IN THE 1900s

"It seems to me that it is entirely proper to start a Zionist State around Jerusalem and [that] the Jews be given control of Palestine," wrote President Theodore Roosevelt (1901–1909).

After World War I, President Woodrow Wilson (1913–1921) supported the Balfour Declaration as England initially tried to make Palestine the Jewish homeland. Wilson responded, "The allied nations with the fullest concurrence of our government and people are agreed that in Palestine shall be laid the foundations of a Jewish Commonwealth."[11]

Though advised against it, Wilson remembered the Bible teachings of his father and grandfather, who were Presbyterian preachers. He cried: "To think that I, the son of the manse [parsonage], should be able to help restore the Holy Land to its people." Wilson also met with William Blackstone, a Christian Zionist and an activist who had appealed to President Wilson for the restoration of the Jews to their homeland.[12]

"It is impossible for one who has studied at all the services of the Hebrew people to avoid the faith that they will one day be restored to their historic national home and there enter on a new and yet greater phase of their contribution to the advance of humanity," said President Warren Harding.[13]

In 1922, President Harding signed the first public resolution passed by Congress to advocate a Jewish homeland in Palestine. However, Harding also supported the restrictive Jewish immigration quota that later cost the lives of so many refugees from the Holocaust.

President Calvin Coolidge (1923–1929) had "sympathy with the deep and intense longing which finds such fine expression in the Jewish National Homeland in Palestine."[14] He paid tribute to the Jews who helped finance the American Revolution: "The Jews themselves, of whom a considerable number were already scattered throughout the colonies, were true to the teachings of their prophets. The Jewish faith is predominantly the faith of liberty."[15]

As the twentieth century progressed and the world required oil for their cars and planes, sympathies changed. The need for the oil gushing up from the Middle East Arab countries began to outweigh Americans' love for God's Word! Loyalties switched to the new royalty of the emerging Arab states.

"I am confident out of these tragic events will come greater security and greater safeguards for the future, under which the steady rehabilitation of the Palestine as a true homeland will be even more assured," said President Herbert Hoover in 1929.[16] In an address to the newly formed American Palestine Committee, Hoover wished to "add my expression to the sentiment among our people in favor of the realization of the age-old aspirations of the Jewish people for the restoration of their national homeland."[17]

Throughout the rest of the chapters, I have integrated into the text the more recent history of the relationship of American presidents and Israel, with a special focus on President Franklin Roosevelt, Harry Truman, and Lyndon Johnson in the chapter "The Key Roles of Three Presidents."

# 3

# *Is God Done*
# With Israel?

W hat's all the fuss about Israel? We're prayer warriors. We're soldiers in the army of God. We're powerful worshipers. We're happy in our churches. Why should we care about Israel?

Does God still care about Israel? Does He still perform supernatural miracles to help her, as in the days of Moses or King David? If the Bible stories are true, did God stop doing what He did in biblical times when the writing of the Bible was finished? Do all the promises and blessings belong to the Church now, as some say?

Orthodox rabbis believe that God created everything and then went back to heaven, leaving us to fend for ourselves. But if God does interact in our world today, wouldn't a miracle be proof of His favor? If an army won a battle by a miracle, wouldn't it prove that God was on their side?

God was definitely on Israel's side back in Old Testament times. Has He changed sides since then? Has God changed His mind and turned His back on His promises to Israel? Were the promises to be for Israel forever, or were they temporary?

*God is not a man, that he should lie, nor a son of man,*
*that he should change his mind. Does he speak and then not*
*act? Does he promise and not fulfill?*
NUMBERS 23:19

*He who is the Glory of Israel does not lie or change his mind;*
*for he is not a man, that he should change his mind.*
1 SAMUEL 15:29

*Jesus Christ is the same yesterday and today and forever.*
HEBREWS 13:8

*Every good and perfect gift is from above, coming down*
*from the Father of the heavenly lights, who does not*
*change like shifting shadows.*
JAMES 1:17

In the *Tenach* (the Hebrew Bible, also known as the Old Testament), God chose a nation of people who descended from Abraham through his son Isaac. He chose them to act out His plan to bring the whole world to Him! In the Hebrew year 2761 (give or take three to four years), Abraham's descendant was born in David's city, to be the Jewish Messiah who would accomplish that plan. (See Isaiah 9:6–7; Luke 3:23–34.)

In the twenty-first century, many have forgotten that believing in Yeshua (Jesus) was originally a Jewish thing to do. It still is. How did the Jewishness of believing in the Messiah and the importance of Israel fade from our awareness? Did it fade from God's awareness?

Certainly not. It is God's End-Time plan, and Israel has a prominent part to play that cannot be avoided. As we view modern history, never has a country had more press coverage and interest throughout the world than this tiny nation. It is interesting that in the mountain range next to *Beth El* (which means "house of God") in Israel, we find a satellite photo showing the formation of the Hebrew letter *Shem*. It is as though God's name is literally stamped on the land He has chosen as His own.

Although over 70 percent of the Jewish people in Israel are secular, this fact does not deter the Lord from calling Jerusalem "the apple of his eye" (Zechariah 2:8). He will fulfill what He has planned in spite of those who wish to carve up this precious land and divide what He has brought together as a whole.

## MISSING: JEWISH ROOTS

We're all missing something. It's something Yeshua had. The 12 disciples had it. The apostle Paul definitely had it. Today, very few Christians still have it.

It's our Jewish roots.

Yeshua and His disciples were Jewish; so were most of the crowds who followed Him, the leaders who argued with Him, and most of the people He healed.

It never occurred to the writers of the Gospels to tell us to continue the Feasts and the *Shabbat* (Sabbath). After all, they were fully covered in the *Torah*, the Five Books of Moses or Pentateuch. Why would anyone forget them?

The *Shabbat* (rest) is the seventh day of the Jewish week and a day of rest in Judaism. It is observed from sundown Friday until the appearance of three stars in the sky on Saturday night.

The *Yom Tov* Feast (good day) is a day or series of days observed by Jews as a holy or secular commemoration of an important event in Jewish history.

The seven biblical Jewish feasts are: Passover (*Pesach*), Unleavened Bread (*Chag Hamotzi*), First Fruits (*Yom habikkurim*), Pentecost (*Shavu'ot*), Trumpets *(Yom Teru'ah)*, Atonement *(Yom Kippur)*, and Tabernacles (*Sukkot*).

At first everyone who followed Yeshua was Jewish. It was the fulfillment of Bible prophecy. The question then was not, "How can you be Jewish and believe in Jesus?" but, "How can a Gentile believe in the Jewish Messiah?" The early believers didn't know what to do with the Gentiles who were putting their faith in Yeshua!

> *I have other sheep that are not of this sheep pen.*
> *I must bring them also. They too will listen to my voice,*
> *and there shall be one flock and one shepherd.*
>
> JOHN 10:16

Here Yeshua gave us an early hint that Gentiles would be saved. During His three-year ministry, He ministered to only a few Gentiles, such as the centurion's servant, the Samaritan woman, who was partly Jewish, and the demoniac.

After Yeshua's death and resurrection, God started to bring Gentiles to salvation. It started with Peter and the vision of the sheet in Acts 10. The unclean animals on the sheet represented Gentiles, not food. God had to do some convincing to get Peter to visit a Gentile home, as the rabbis said that going into a Gentile home would make a Jew unclean. With that visit, the Gentile Cornelius was saved and filled with the Holy Spirit, along with his relatives and close friends. They were subsequently baptized.

In Acts 15, the apostles and elders in Jerusalem had a meeting to decide what was expected from the many Gentiles who were coming to faith in the Jewish God. They decided that Gentiles would not have to be circumcised, but should observe certain stipulations:

> *It is my judgment, therefore, that we should not*
> *make it difficult for the Gentiles who are turning to God.*
> *Instead we should write to them, telling them to abstain*
> *from food polluted by idols, from sexual immorality,*
> *from the meat of strangled animals and from blood.*
>
> ACTS 15:19–20

As each generation passed on the new "Gentilized" Christianity, the Jewishness slipped away. The gospel became Gentile! Satan was at work to push Israel out of the equation.

How did Satan steal the gospel from Israel? Who was his agent on earth?

## CONSTANTINE

Emperor Constantine, who ruled the Roman Empire from 306–337, wanted to get control of the pagans in Rome. He declared that Christianity would be the official Roman religion. In order to attract them, he transformed their pagan feasts and celebrations into "Christian" ones.

Constantine convened several councils to unite the Church and eliminate heresy. The infamous Nicean Council met in 325 to counter Arianism, a false doctrine that questioned the divinity of Yeshua and of the Holy Spirit.[18] The decisions reached at Nicaea went far beyond the nature of the Trinity and into the area of driving out all Jewishness from the church.

Jews were forbidden to celebrate *Shabbat* or the *Yom Tov* (the feasts). They were forced to accept Jesus and were tortured and killed if they continued doing anything Jewish. Burning Jews at the stake was a favorite Roman spectator sport.[19]

There is some question whether Constantine himself ever became a Christian. Although he was the first Roman emperor to legalize Christianity, he may have done it to bring order to the poor masses and not because of any personal faith. Constantine was finally baptized as he was dying. Had he ever made a sincere profession of faith, he would have been baptized then.[20]

The holy days that Yeshua tied all His ministry to were converted! Pagan holidays were adapted and made Christian.

Saturnalia, the pagan observance of the winter solstice, became Christmas. Yeshua was probably not born in December but in October at Succoth. Jerusalem and nearby Bethlehem were crowded because it was a pilgrim feast, so all the Jewish men had to travel there.

Ishtar, the pagan fertility rites in early spring, was changed into Easter. It was loosely tied to Passover, but eclipsed the significance of Yeshua as the Passover Lamb.

Sabbath observance was changed to Sunday, based on the misunderstanding of Paul at Troas:

*On the first day of the week we came together to break bread.*
*Paul spoke to the people and, because he intended to leave*
*the next day, kept on talking until midnight. There were many*
*lamps in the upstairs room where we were meeting.*
ACTS 20:7–8

This prayer meeting took place at night, not on Sunday morning! The first day of the week started at sundown on Saturday evening, as it still does in Israel. The believers were meeting for the *Havdallah* service, to mark the close of *Shabbat*. That is why the room was all lit up. That is when they took the offering for the needy in Jerusalem. That's why Paul preached until so late at night that a young boy fell asleep and fell out of the window.

Another time, Paul took up a collection for the believers in Jerusalem:

*Now about the collection for God's people:*
*Do what I told the Galatian churches to do. On the first day*
*of every week, each one of you should set aside a sum of*
*money in keeping with his income, saving it up, so that*
*when I come no collections will have to be made.*
1 CORINTHIANS 16:1–2

The first day, as above, was probably the *Havdallah* service on Saturday night. Jewish people did not handle money on the *Shabbat*, so the collection was made afterward.

Without the correct understanding of the two passages about the first day, it is easy to misinterpret the text as saying that the early Church changed their Sabbath to Sunday. Clearly, Paul never intended to disobey the fourth commandment by changing the Sabbath! The Sabbath is the seventh day of the week; in Israel it is the name of that day. The week is: First Day, Second Day,....*Shabbat*.

*But the seventh day is a Sabbath to the LORD your God.*
EXODUS 20:10

As a result of Rome's heavy hand and the new pagan converts, the Church started to forget its Jewish roots. Church leaders began to teach that the Church had replaced Israel. Was that true?

Why is there so much misunderstanding and wrong interpretation? Why did Satan steal the gospel from the Jews?

Psalm 118:25–26 describes Yeshua's procession into Jerusalem on Palm Sunday:

> *O LORD, save us;*
> *O LORD, grant us success.*
> *Blessed is he who comes in the name of the LORD.*
> *From the house of the LORD we bless you.*
> *The Lord is God, and he has made his light shine upon us.*
> *With boughs in hand, join in the festal procession*
> *up to the horns of the altar.*
> PSALM 118:25–27

> *Bind the sacrifice with cords, even unto the horns of the altar.*
> PSALM 118:27 KJV

Yeshua's arrival in Jerusalem for Passover was prophesied in Psalm 118. The people recognized that this was happening and sang verse 25: "LORD, save us!" "Hosanna!" Knowing that the people heralded His arrival with Psalm 118, Yeshua said at the Last Supper (the Passover *Seder*):

> *For I tell you, you will not see me again until you say,*
> *"Blessed is he who comes in the name of the Lord"*
> *[Baruch ha ba, ba Shem Adonai].*
> MATTHEW 23:39

They greeted Him this time with *Baruch ha ba, ba Shem Adonai*, and He will not come again until He is summoned with *Baruch ha ba, ba Shem Adonai!* Israel has to recognize Him as Messiah, just as they did that Passion Week, before He will come to them again.

Satan heard this. Satan's mission ever since has been to prevent the Jewish people from recognizing Yeshua as their Messiah. This will keep Yeshua from returning as He said, thereby proving Him a liar. If God is a liar, then all of His Word is untrue, and no one should believe in Him.

Jewish salvations and the restoration of Jewish roots to the Church will foil Satan's plan. God will fulfill His.

> *So shall my word be that goeth forth out of my mouth: it shall not return unto me void, but it shall accomplish that which I please, and it shall prosper in the thing whereto I sent it.*
>
> ISAIAH 55:11 KJV

## REPLACEMENT THEOLOGY

Replacement theology states that the Church is Israel and all the biblical promises to Israel now apply to the Church. It essentially teaches that the Church has replaced Israel in God's plan. Adherents of replacement theology believe the Jews are no longer God's chosen people, and God does not have specific future plans for the nation of Israel. Israel is cast aside, even hated by God.

Replacement theology is described by Zionists as "a bigoted doctrine of the Medieval Church," and it is connected with anti-Semitism and specifically the promotion of the charge of *Deicide*—that the Jews are blamed for the crucifixion. This charge from the Medieval Church led to numerous genocides against the Jewish people in various countries. The Inquisition, the Crusades, and eventually the Holocaust happened because people were convinced (by the clergy) that they were obeying God's will by killing Jews! The Inquisition got its name because they were questioning, inquiring of Jews whether they were Christians and whether they stopped all Jewish practices!

During the Middle Ages (from the fifth century through the sixteenth century), the Church had morphed into the Catholic Church. Most of the priests and bishops were not born again and were not led by the Holy Spirit. They were ambitious, politically motivated men who were hungry for power. They controlled the people by teaching them lies and instilling hatred toward the Jews. They misinterpreted the Bible, with a special emphasis in Romans 9–11 and Galatians 2. The common people were ignorant and purposely not taught to read. Having no idea what the Bible said, the people looked to the clergy to interpret it for them. The teachings they received led to the Dark Ages, the Inquisition, and the Crusades.

For a thorough chronicle of the atrocities done to the Jewish people in the name of Christ, read *Our Hands Are Stained With Blood* by Dr. Michael Brown.

Unfortunately, replacement theology is still being propagated in some theological seminaries and Bible colleges. Many trained pastors emerge from these higher institutions of learning and are convinced of this untruth. Consequently, the churches they pastor receive the same lies that have been perpetuated for centuries.

If Satan can replace the ideas of God with lies and man's misunderstandings, he will win. This will not be, however, for the Lord's truth will triumph in the end. In these past few years there has been a concerted effort by many international ministries to defeat this lie.

## DUAL COVENANT

Replacement theology usually goes hand in hand with another false doctrine called "dual covenant"—a theological term found in contemporary inter-religious circles that teaches that Jews may simply keep the Law of Moses, because of the "everlasting covenant" (Genesis 17:13) between Abraham and God, whereas Gentiles (those not Jews or Jewish proselytes) must convert to Christianity.

Dual covenant theology was originated by Rabbi Moshe Ben-Maimon (1135–1204) and pioneered in the twentieth century by the Jewish philosopher Franz Rosenzweig (1886–1929). It may be understood as a modern variant of the Talmudic doctrine stating that Jews are bound by the Torah, but Gentiles share in the world to come if they obey the seven Noahide Laws given after the flood to Noah for all mankind—prohibitions against idolatry, murder, incest, theft, blasphemy, and eating the flesh of a living animal; and the positive command to promote justice, i.e., to institute government.

Since the Christian view, dual covenant theology has been elaborated by liberal Christian theologians such as Reinhold Niebuhr and James Parkes. According to David H. Stern, Jesus' word is not for Jews but for Gentiles. For example, in John 14:6 where Jesus said, "I am the way, the truth, and the life. No one comes to the Father except through me," they would say it should be understood in this way: "I am the way, the truth, and the life; and no Gentile comes to the Father except through me."

---

*Who are Israelites, to whom belongs the adoption as sons, and the glory and the covenants and the giving of the Law and the temple service and the promises...*
ROMANS 9:4 NASB

*Even us, whom He also called, not from among Jews only, but also from among Gentiles.*
ROMANS 9:24 NASB

*That means that there is no difference between Jew and Gentile—Adonai is the same for everyone, rich toward everyone who calls on him, since everyone who calls on the name of Adonai will be delivered.*
ROMANS 10:12–13 CJB

*For just as you once were disobedient to God, but now have been shown mercy because of their disobedience, so these also now have been disobedient, that because of the mercy shown to you they also may now be shown mercy. For God has shut up all in disobedience so that He may show mercy to all.*
ROMANS 11:30–32 NASB

*As for those who seemed to be important—whatever they were makes no difference to me; God does not judge by external appearance—those men added nothing to my message. On the contrary, they saw that I had been entrusted with the task of preaching the gospel to the Gentiles, just as Peter had been to the Jews. For God, who was at work in the ministry of Peter as an apostle to the Jews, was also at work in my ministry as an apostle to the Gentiles. James, Peter and John, those reputed to be pillars, gave me and Barnabas the right hand of fellowship when they recognized the grace given to me. They agreed that we should go to the Gentiles, and they to the Jews.*

GALATIANS 2:6–9

Many Christians engage in dialogue with Jewish people. They think that by talking they will receive the blessing for those who bless Israel. They also give lots of money to ministries that bring Jews to Israel from Russia and Ethiopia. It doesn't bother them that these ministries will not share the gospel with the people they help. Why doesn't that bother them? Because they believe that Jews do not need the gospel!

The doctrine of dual covenant says that Israel has salvation through the Torah and through doing good works. They believe that Israel does not need salvation through the Messiah, because they have the Torah. They can give money to Israel and talk to Israel's leaders, but don't offend them by discussing Jesus!

If Jews don't need Yeshua, then why did He spend His whole earthly ministry addressing them and debating their leaders? Almost every healing was of a Jewish person. He fulfilled all the Messianic prophecies in the Scriptures. He was the Jewish Messiah who came to the Jewish people, who were waiting for Him.

The Old Testament says a lot about salvation and atonement and how to get them. The Old Testament is addressing Jewish people when it says that all have sinned and need to do something about it!

*What is man, that he could be pure, or one born of woman, that he could be righteous?*

JOB 15:14

*All have turned aside, they have together become corrupt; there is no one who does good, not even one.*

PSALM 14:3

*Who can say, "I have kept my heart pure;*
*I am clean and without sin"?*
PROVERBS 20:9

*We all, like sheep, have gone astray, each of us*
*has turned to his own way; and the LORD has laid on*
*him the iniquity of us all.*
ISAIAH 53:6

*When they sin against you—*
*for there is no one who does not sin.*
1 KINGS 8:46

*There is not a righteous man on earth who*
*does what is right and never sins.*
ECCLESIASTES 7:20

We are more familiar with the New Testament versions of these verses:

*For all have sinned and fall short of the glory of God,*
*and are justified freely by his grace through the*
*redemption that came by Christ Jesus.*
ROMANS 3:23–24

*If we claim to be without sin, we deceive*
*ourselves and the truth is not in us.*
1 JOHN 1:8

You can argue that these New Testament verses apply to Gentiles, but when they were written, most of the believers were Jewish.

All men and women are equal in God's eyes. Sin separates people from God, whether Jewish or Gentile. When our sins are forgiven by God through the Messiah's blood, we become Jew and Gentile together, or One New Man, as described in Ephesians 2.

We must remember that there are very good reasons to convince Jewish people that there is but one road to salvation. I repeat: If Satan can deceive those who are chosen by God, Yeshua's return will be delayed. The Jews are waiting for a Messiah to return, but not One with nail-pierced hands and feet. Jesus said one day they will look up and see whom they have pierced and cry out *Baruch Ha Ba Bashem Adonai*. To have another way of salvation besides through Jesus makes it very easy for a Jew to accept. However, there is no other way to the Father except through the Son (John 3:16).

## WHO IS ISRAEL?

If we are to bless Israel and pray for Israel, we must clarify: Who exactly is Israel?

Does Israel consist of the physical inhabitants of *Eretz Israel*, the land of Israel? Is Israel all the Jewish people spread throughout the world? Is the Church now Israel? Or are Jews who believe in Yeshua (Messianic Jews) Israel?

The answer is: All of the above!

The literal country of Israel and its inhabitants are the natural Israel. The *galut* (dispersion) of Jewish people in many nations is also natural Israel. The Church is spiritual Israel, descendants of Abraham by faith. Jewish believers, the few who follow Yeshua, are the remnant whose numbers have been increasing over the past few decades more than ever before.

A better question than "Who is Israel?" is: Who inherits the flow of God? Who are God's hands and feet on the earth today? Who is the Israel of God?

The better answer is that spiritual Israel is the One New Man: Jews and Gentiles following Yeshua together.

We see all of Israel being important to God, and that ultimately each effects the other. We cannot try to delineate one from the other, for they are all part of the same whole. Israel is God's spiritual timepiece, and He uses those movements to effect the world. Time and time again we see the comparisons throughout history as this is incorporated. You will find many examples of what I am explaining in later chapters in this book.

Nowhere in history has a property been so disputed and abused as the little nation of Israel. This tiny nation was not so small when it was originally given over to Abraham and later to Joshua and the 12 tribes. Unfortunately, through time and wars and the politics of kings, presidents, and prime ministers, it has been carved up to the present size of today. You will find more information in the last chapter on the true geographical size of this nation.

You have to realize that for the nation of Israel to be in existence is a miracle in and of itself. For just like the Assyrians and the Babylonians of ancient history, Israel was no longer in existence. Only God could have resurrected this nation after disappearing for 2,000 years. No matter whether you believe the Bible or not, the fact of the matter stands that this miracle is a reality and was stated in the Bible to transpire.

# ONE NEW MAN

*For he himself is our peace, who has made the two one*
*and has destroyed the barrier, the dividing wall of hostility...*
*His purpose was to create in himself one new man*
*out of the two, thus making peace.*
Ephesians 2:14–15

*Jews and Gentiles one in Messiah,*
*one in Yeshua, one in the olive tree,*
*Jews and Gentiles one in Messiah, one in Yeshua's love.*
Joel Chernoff, from the song "Jews and Gentiles"

During the book of Acts and for approximately 150 years after, it was quite normal for Jewish and Gentile believers to celebrate the Sabbath and the feasts. Remember God said these were His feasts. He called them a holy convocation to come and meet with Him.

After 2,000 years of anti-Semitism, most of the Christian world has divorced itself from anything Jewish. A Jewish person sees nothing appealing or enticing about going into a church. To him, church is an alien, hostile place associated with murder and persecution. Newly saved Jewish people are told they are no longer Jewish and are now Christians.

According to a senior rabbi from the North American Messianic Association, one Southern Baptist pastor told a new Jewish believer who was about to be baptized, "We're gonna wash that Jew right out of you!" The young man left and never returned, turning his back on Yeshua.

There are certainly exceptions. More and more churches today are making efforts to restore their Jewish roots, but they are a minority, especially among mainline denominations.

Many young Jewish baby boomers became believers in Yeshua during the Jesus Movement during the 1960s and 1970s. Messianic congregations developed to satisfy the longing for a Jewish expression of their faith in the Jewish Messiah. Organizations arose to organize the congregations, such as the MJAA (Messianic Jewish Association of America) and the UMJC (Union of Messianic Jewish Congregations).

Just as the Church strayed from its Jewish roots, so the Messianic Movement started veering off course. There is too much emphasis on how many members are Jewish and too little interaction with other churches. Most Messianic congregations keep separate from most churches.

There would be no need for Messianic congregations if churches restored in their worship and services more of what God had established in the book of Leviticus. If churches kept all their traditions, whether they have pagan roots or not, but simply added *Shabbat* service and the Feasts, that would be good start.

What does all this mean to us? Simply that the Lord is coming back for one bride without spot, blemish, or wrinkle. Not a Jewish-believing bride and a Gentile-believing bride—that is a bride with two heads. God is not into monsters. No, He wants the wild olive branch and the natural olive branch to be grafted into one vine who is Yeshua. Then the one new man will be formed in both, according to the Scriptures, and they will become one bride for Him.

# 4

# *The Look of the* Middle East Today

The history of the Middle East has been shaped by some unlikely events. The shape of today's Arab world grew out of the promises made during World War I by a British officer to Muslims from western Arabia.

## LAWRENCE OF ARABIA

At the outbreak of WWI, Lieutenant Colonel T. E. Lawrence was sent to the Arabian Desert by the British to enlist the help of the nomadic Arab tribes living there. Lawrence's mission was to unite them into an army to stage raids against the Ottoman Turks, so that England could gain control of the Middle East.

Lawrence gathered together only a few tribes, who attacked and pillaged Turkish supply lines and attacked Aqaba, a coastal town in the far south of what is now Jordan. Then they all raced to Damascus, entering the city just ahead of the British army. The principal tribe was the Hashemite, who served as guardians of the holy Muslim sites of Mecca and Medina.[21]

Lawrence's mission had only minimal success. Lasting impact came from something unexpected—a popular legend created by news articles written by the imaginative American journalist Lowell Thomas, one of the most popular reporters of the day. Thomas heard about a British captain working with the Arab tribes out in the vast desert. It smelled like a good story, so he found Lawrence and his Arab comrades and followed them around as they blew up trains and raided supply lines. Thomas transformed an obscure, ineffective operation into page-one news by sending home thrilling stories and posed pictures. He made a thrilling, romantic international hero out of Lawrence, dubbing him "Lawrence of Arabia." Later David Lean's Oscar-winning movie, *Lawrence of Arabia*, starring Peter O'Toole, grew from those stories. Most of us think the movie was true historical fact, but it was only a colorful myth.

After the war, Lawrence was trying to reward his Arab friends by having the British give them countries of their own. England would have refused were it not for the pressure caused by Lawrence's fame.

The following excerpt comes from Jack Wheeler's October 2, 2002 article, "Curse of T. E. Lawrence's Promise: The Phony Nation of Iraq" in the *Daily Reckoning of New Orleans*:

> *By the time the Treaty of Sevres was negotiated in 1920, with Lawrence in attendance and the media mob hanging on his every word, the British felt compelled to keep Lawrence's promise to the chieftains of an Arab tribe called the Hashemite. The political structure of the Middle East today is the result of that promise. The Treaty of Sevres permitted the British to seize pieces of the Ottoman Empire, which had ruled the Middle East for centuries, but joined the Germans in WWI. Instead of British colonies, the pieces were called League of Nations' mandates, for which the Brits needed puppet rulers. At the time the British, Dutch, and American*

*petroleum companies were very interested in being able to control the Middle East oil potential.*

To make a long story short, Lawrence was able to persuade the British—with the pressure of his media popularity helping—to put together three provinces of the old Ottoman Empire and make one country called Iraq and give it to a Hashemite prince named Feisal. The people of these three provinces have hated one another for centuries. Apart from a ruthless dictator, such as Saddam Hussein, no one could keep them together.

Lawrence also was able to persuade the British to betray their mandate to create a homeland for the Jews. When the Saudis drove the Hashemite out of Mecca and Medina, he persuaded the British to give Prince Abdullah the land mandated to the Jews known as Trans-Jordan as a consolation prize. Today, that is known as the Royal Kingdom of Jordan.

The British were not in favor of the Jewish people, and at the time of ratification in 1948 in the United Nations, they voted against Israel becoming a state. It was well known that the British did not favor any immigration by the Jews into Palestine and prevented it at every level.

Myth and publicity created to sell newspapers helped to form the mess in the Middle East. Broken promises and betrayal by Israel's top leaders kept it going.

## WHO ARE ISRAEL'S ENEMIES?

Israel's enemies are all the neighboring Arab countries, especially Iran, Iraq, and Syria. Israel enjoys an uneasy peace with Egypt and Jordan. Lebanon's government is controlled by the Syrian Hezbollah. Israel's most direct enemy is the undeclared state of Palestine.

## WHO IS PALESTINE?

Calling Israel by the name of "Palestine" is an attempt by the British to belittle and mock Israel's claim to the land. The name is based on Israel's ancient archrival, the Philistines.

At the 1919 Paris Peace Conference, Emir Faisal bin Hussein and Chaim Weizmann met to discuss Jewish settlement in Palestine. The head of the Arab delegation, Emir Faisal, was about to become the king of Syria. He ruled for a short time during 1920 and then was the king of Iraq from 1921–1933. Weizmann was the head of the World Zionist Organization. The two leaders signed the Faisal-Weizmann Agreement.[22]

Despite later complaints by Arab nations about the refugee problem, neither man addressed those concerns in this agreement. Worse, they both spoke of the Arabs living in Palestine with disdain:

*Weizmann had called them treacherous, arrogant,
uneducated, and greedy and had complained to the British
that the system in Palestine did not take into account the fact
that there is a fundamental qualitative difference between Jew
and Arab. After his meeting with Faisal, Weizmann reported
that Faisal was "contemptuous of the Palestinian Arabs whom
he doesn't even regard as Arabs."[23]*

No Arab country would take in the Palestinian Arab refugees, but they all used them as propaganda before the world, calling them a "dispossessed people."

## THE PLO

The Palestinian Liberation Organization was started in 1964 by Yasser Arafat within Israel, but with the backing of Egypt. Its main purpose was the liberation of Palestine. However, at that time, all of the so-called Palestinian territories in the West Bank and Gaza were in Arab hands. So what could liberating Palestine have meant, other than the destruction of Israel?

During the 1967 War, members of the PLO fled to Jordan with many Arab residents of Israel. The PLO's hostile behavior in Jordan caused King Hussein to launch the Black September attack in 1970. Many of the PLO were killed. The leaders fled to Lebanon where they established training camps. It was there that modern terrorism was born and launched throughout the world.

Among the PLO's heinous adventures were the kidnap and murder of Israeli athletes at the 1972 Munich Olympics and the 1985 hijacking of the cruise ship *Achille Lauro*, where the terrorists shot an old Jewish man in a wheelchair and threw his body overboard. Numerous bombing and hijackings made the headlines year after year.

The PLO is synonymous with Palestine. All the peace talks center around their demands to have their own country within Israel or instead of Israel.

# 5

# *Israel's* Prime Ministers

D oesn't it seem as though the prime ministers of Israel get elected based on their promises to be tough? Don't each of them say they wouldn't negotiate with the Palestinians until they comply with past agreements? Don't they say they would encourage and protect settlers in outlying areas? What happens to them after they get elected?

Why do the Israeli prime ministers change the policies that get them elected? Why do they break their campaign promises and betray their people? Do they conceal their real agenda in order to get elected? Do they give in to pride, hoping to make their mark on history by being the hero who finally achieves peace, regardless of the cost?

Shouldn't the leaders of Israel be familiar with the Hebrew Scriptures? How could any leader of Israel give away one inch of God-given land? Their behavior boggles the mind. They seem to act against Israel's best interests. It often looks like treason!

Most of these leaders were resistance fighters and zealous Zionists in the pioneer days of Palestine. Some were terrorists, some killed British officials, and some were socialists. How did these hawks become such doves?

How can a person who is smart enough to rise to the top office believe that appeasement of the Arabs will bring peace? Why don't they get it? Only victory over an enemy brings peace! Appeasement makes Israel look weak. War after war has proven that only military strength stops an aggressive enemy.

Then, when each candidate runs for office, he or she points to the broken promises of the incumbent. When the candidate wins, watch him break the very same promises right away!

To a large extent, the prime minister turnarounds resulted from pressure from U.S. presidents and the U.S. State Department to accept whatever the Arabs pretended to agree to. Most of these agreements defy common sense and serve to hamstring Israel. But each U.S. president got to look like a great statesman!

Also, the prime ministers may have been reluctant to rule over areas with large Arab populations. It's easier to govern Jewish areas!

Let's look at each Israeli prime minister to see what they said before the elections and after.

# DAVID BEN-GURION (1948–1954, 1955–1963)

David Ben-Gurion said the Zionists "would fight the war as if there was no White Paper and fight the White Paper as if there was no war." One of the early Zionist heroes, he helped establish Israel as a nation. Before 1948, he led the Jewish Agency, which served as a government for the Jews in Palestine under the British mandate. When Israel became a nation, he became its leader.

During his first term as prime minister, he set up agencies and cities and created an army out of the various resistance groups that had fought against British rule. The Israeli Defense Force (IDF) united the *Irgun*, led by Menachem Begin, and the *Haganah*, led by Ben-Gurion. The *Haganah* had been an illegal arm of the Jewish Agency. At that time, Ben-Gurion always advanced Israel's best interests.

For two years, Ben-Gurion retired from politics, but returned to office in 1955 for another eight years. In the interim, Israel was led by Prime Minister Moshe Sharett.

During his second term, Ben-Gurion changed from a leader who encouraged settlement in the territories to one who gave away the Sinai Peninsula to end the war with Egypt. Many former supporters were aghast. It was the first land-for-peace giveaway for the new nation of Israel.

In 1953, David Ben-Gurion said to Ariel Sharon: "Let me first tell you one thing: It doesn't matter what the world says about Israel; it doesn't matter what they say about us anywhere else. The only thing that matters is that we can exist here on the land of our forefathers. And unless we show the Arabs that there is a high price to pay for murdering Jews, we won't survive."[24]

## MOSHE SHARETT (1954–1955)

Moshe Sharett was also a leader in the Jewish Agency. He led negotiations between the British and the Zionist leaders to create the state of Israel. Then he brokered the 1949 Armistice Agreement to end the 1948 war.

Under Sharett, Israeli intelligence staged a failed mission that tainted Sharett's leadership. It was known as the Lavon Affair, named for Pinhas Livon, the defense minister who had to resign because of it.

In 1954, Britain managed the Suez Canal as a neutral zone. The U.S. was pressuring Britain to withdraw. Israel feared that withdrawal would embolden Egypt's Nasser to blockade the canal as he was threatening. Operation Susannah was Israel's mission to bomb targets in Egypt so the British would stay there. The operation was bungled so badly that the inquiry never resolved what happened!

As prime minister, Sharett wanted to negotiate with the Arabs, a tactic that always proves fruitless. Ben-Gurion did not agree and ran for office again, forcing Sharett out.

## LEVI ESHKOL (1963–1969)

Levi Eshkol was handpicked by David Ben-Gurion to succeed him as prime minister. He brought Israel into a closer alliance with the U.S. as President Lyndon Johnson helped Israel arm itself against the threats coming from Egypt. Weapons from the U.S. helped Israel win the 1967 Six-Day War. This was a shining moment in U.S.-Israeli relations!

The Israelis lost confidence in Eshkol as he seemed to shrink back from Nasser's taunts by not attacking Egypt right away. He was waiting as long as he could to build up Israel's stash of weapons. His strategy worked out, but people did not give him the credit for the swift victory over Egypt. Defense Minister Moshe Dayan became the war hero while Levi Eshkol was labeled as a wimp.

In 1969, Eshkol died in office of a heart attack.

## GOLDA MEIR (1969–1974)

Golda Meir replaced Eshkol after his death. She led Israel during its strongest season. Israel was a strong warrior whose army and intelligence network evoked a fearful respect from Arab enemies. It was a time of strong leadership and good relations with the U.S.

Meir was one of Israel's founders, a leader of the Labor Socialist Zionist movement that grew into a nation. She signed the Declaration of Establishment, and in her 1948 visit to the U.S., she raised 50 million dollars to defend Israel from the Arab attacks.

In 1972, the PLO launched world terrorism by murdering 11 Israeli athletes at the 1972 Munich Olympics. Disappointed with the response from the U.S. and the world, Israel's leaders took matters into their own hands. They launched assassins from *Mossad*, Israel's intelligence agency, to kill every terrorist who played a part in Black September. Those were the days when Israel reacted to aggression with *chutzpah*!

By 1973, Israel's military preparedness had degraded. Overconfident after the easy win in 1967, Meir ignored warnings and the buildup by Syria. The lady statesman turned Israel from the mighty warrior into the sitting duck!

Golda Meir provided numerous great quotes:

*To be or not to be is not a question of compromise. Either you be or you don't be.... If we are criticized because we do*

*not bow because we cannot compromise on the question
"To be or not to be," it is because we have decided that,
come what may, we are and we will be.*

*There cannot be quiet on one side of the border and
shelling on the other. We will either have peace on both
sides or trouble on both sides.*

*If we lose a war, that's the end forever, and we
disappear from the earth. If one fails to understand this,
then one fails to understand obstinacy. We intend to remain
alive. Our neighbors want to see us dead. This is not a
question that leaves much room for compromise.*

*Our secret weapon: No alternative.*

*Do the Arabs need another land?
They already have fourteen. We have only one.*

## YITZHAK RABIN (1974–1977)

Rabin was leader in the *Haganah*. In the 1948 War, he led the army in Jerusalem and in the Negev desert against Egypt. In 1964, he was the leader of IDF (Israel Defense Forces) and led it in the 1967 War.

Rabin's greatest moment was his part in the Operation Entebbe—a hostage-rescue mission carried out by the IDF at Entebbe Airport in Uganda that took place on the night of July 3 and early morning of July 4, 1976, when members of the militant organizations, Revolutionary Cells and the Popular Front for the Liberation of Palestine, hijacked the Air France Flight 139.

Originally named Operation Thunderball by the IDF, it was later renamed Operation Yonatan in memory of the *Sayeret Matkal* commander Lieutenant Colonel Yonatan Netanyahu, the older brother of Benjamin Netanyahu, who was the only commando killed in the fighting. The IDF acted on intelligence provided by Israeli secret agency *Mossad*. All the hijackers, three hostages, and 45 Ugandan soldiers were killed, and five Israeli commandos were wounded. A fourth hostage was murdered by Ugandan army officers at a nearby hospital.

Read more about Prime Minister Rabin in his second term: 1992–1995.

## SHIMON PERES (1977)

Peres served as prime minister three times, more often than anyone else. Yitzhak Shamir and Yitzhak Rabin served twice.

Like President Gerald Ford, Shimon Peres was the only prime minister who was never elected. In 1977, Peres succeeded Yitzhak Rabin after he resigned. Peres held the post a short time until he lost that year's election to Menachem Begin.

Read more about Peres during his next two terms in office.

## MENACHEM BEGIN (1977–1983)

Orthodox Jew Menachem Begin was a young resistance fighter in pre-1948 British Palestine. He led the *Irgun*, the more militant of the two underground armies. The other group was David Ben-Gurion's *Haganah*.

Until the Camp David Accords of 1978, former terrorist Begin was viewed as a militant hardliner, even a radical. He promoted and encouraged settlements throughout the Sinai and the West Bank. Begin was called the hero of the people, the villain of the government.

In 1981, Begin reverted to his warhorse image by staging Operation Opera, a preemptive air attack on Iraq's nuclear reactor in Tammuz. As usual, the U.N. and even the U.S. condemned the action. However, this explains the Begin doctrine:

*On no account shall we permit an enemy to develop weapons of mass destruction (WMD) against the people of Israel.*

Was this man who stopped Iraq in its tracks in 1982 the same man who shared the 1978 Nobel Peace Prize with Anwar Sadat by giving the Sinai Peninsula to Egypt (again)?

Hardliners Yitzhak Shamir and Ariel Sharon stood against Begin's policy of granting land for peace. In 1982, as the Israeli army (IDF) forcibly evicted settlers from the Yamit settlement, their Movement for Stopping the Withdrawal from Sinai resisted the eviction to the point of violence.

How the tables turned by 2005, when Prime Minister Sharon was the one using the army to evict settlers in Gaza!

Begin's reign also saw Israel get stuck in the quagmire of Lebanon, reminiscent of the U.S. sojourn in Vietnam. To retaliate against Syrian terrorists in Lebanon, Israel invaded Lebanon in 1982. They could not extricate themselves until 2000. During that time, the PLO fled from their bases in Lebanon to set up shop in Tunis, Tunisia.

On the day after the U.N. vote on the 1947 U.N. Partition Plan, Menachem Begin stated:

*The Partition of Palestine is illegal. It will never be recognized.... Jerusalem was and will forever be our capital. Eretz Israel will be restored to the people of Israel. All of it. And forever.*

Soon after Menachem Begin was elected in 1977, the government's foreign policy was stated as follows:

*The Jewish people have unchallengeable, eternal, historic right to the land of Israel [including the West Bank and Gaza Strip], the inheritance of their forefathers* (and he pledged to build rural and urban exclusive Jewish colonies in the West Bank and Gaza Strip).[25]

## YITZHAK SHAMIR (1983–1984)

See Shamir's second term, 1986–1992.

## SHIMON PERES (1984–1986)

As Foreign Minister in 1980, Peres stated that "the option of opening negotiations with the PLO does not really exist." He explained that the PLO has "a number of separate armed factions, is not democratic, and lacks the authority of disciplined leadership."

In 1984, Shimon Peres became prime minister. The two *Knesset* (Israel's congress) parties decided to rotate Israel's leadership. Peres would serve as prime minister for two years, then he would trade places with Foreign Minister Yitzhak Shamir.

## YITZHAK SHAMIR (1986–1992)

Yitzhak Shamir rose to power through violence. Before 1948, Shamir served in the *Irgun* and in a subgroup of the *Irgun*, the militant Stern Group, named after its leader, Avraham Stern. They assassinated British and U.N. officials. Shamir's Stern Group actively negotiated with the Nazis in the 1940s: They would fight for Germany against the British in Palestine, to help Germany take over Europe, in return for the release of all Jews to Palestine!

After Israel's statehood, Shamir became a spy for the *Mossad*. Later he became Chairman of the *Knesset*. There he abstained in the September 1978 vote on the Camp David agreement, and in March 1979, he abstained from voting on the Egyptian peace treaty. He was firmly against negotiating for peace.

How did the militant spy, assassin, and underground fighter take part in the 1989 Peace Initiative and the Madrid Peace Talks in 1991?

How did the freedom fighter sit still in 1991 as Saddam's Scuds rained down on Israel while the U.S. told Israel not to defend itself?

Ironically, Shamir, the hardliner, was voted out of office for his role in negotiating for peace.

## YITZHAK RABIN (1992–1995)

*You do not make peace with friends; you make peace with very unsavory enemies.*[26]

*With the PLO as an organization, I will not negotiate.*

*In 1979, although Labor and the Likud differ in their views on the solution to the Palestinian question, we both oppose in the strongest terms the creation of a Palestinian "mini-state" in the West Bank and the Gaza Strip, first and foremost because it cannot solve anything.... The leaders of the PLO have declared—and I believe them—that they view such a mini-state as but the first phase in the achievement of their so-called secular, democratic Palestine, to be built on the ruins of the State of Israel.*

As prime minister, with less than a year in office under his belt, Rabin did enter into talks with the PLO.

Rabin's great legacy is the Oslo Accords of 1993 (see "The Peace Process" chapter). For his contribution, he shared the 1994 Nobel Peace Prize with Shimon Peres and Yasser Arafat. Thanks to Oslo, the Palestinian Authority was set up and given control of the West Bank and Gaza.

Israeli perception of the Oslo Accords was sharply divided. Some hailed Rabin as a hero, while many labeled him as a traitor who weakened Israel in the eyes of the Arab world and gave away God-given land.

Orthodox activist Yigal Amir was definitely anti-Oslo. On November 4, 1995, he shot and killed the prime minister as he left a peace rally in Tel Aviv celebrating Oslo. Moments before he left the stage, Rabin was singing the song *"Shir Lashalom"* ("Song for Peace"), along with an Israeli singer. The bloody paper with the lyrics that was found in his pocket seemed to say, "Peace only comes with blood!"

After his assassination, Rabin became an icon of Israeli hopes for peace, despite his early days fighting in the *Haganah* and leading the IDF.

## SHIMON PERES (1995–1996)

Shimon Peres was also a *Haganah* leader in the early days of Palestine. He lived on kibbutzs, one of which he established and led. In the *Haganah*, he was in charge of procuring men and guns. He continued to do that after 1948. He rose through government ranks as finance minister, then foreign minister, minister of absorption (of immigrants), as well as minister of transportation, communication, and information.

As defense minister during the 1956 Suez Crisis, Peres was called the mastermind of the 1956 Sinai Campaign for acquiring an advanced French jet fighter, a nuclear reactor, and for forging an alliance between Israel, France, and the U.K. On the dove side, Peres also tried to improve relations with neighboring Arab countries through his vision of a new Middle East.

He and Yitzhak Rabin ran against each other for prime minister several times. Peres kept losing!

Finally, in 1995, Peres was appointed prime minister after Rabin's assassination. During his brief term, Peres helped to popularize the Internet in Israel by having the first prime minister's website.

In 1996, Peres lost to Benjamin Netanyahu by a narrow margin. In 2007, Peres was elected president.

How did Shimon Peres turn from a hawk into a dove? He was a *Haganah* arms supplier; a defense minister procuring advanced weapons for Israel; a protégé of David Ben-Gurion and Moshe Dayan; and a supporter of the settlers in the West Bank in the 1970s.

Yet once he became the party leader in the *Knesset*, Peres talked peace through economic cooperation and territorial compromise on the West Bank and Gaza.

In 1994, Peres won the Nobel Peace Prize along with Rabin and Arafat for their roles in the Oslo Accords. Peres started the Oslo process as foreign minister in 1992 by holding secret meetings with Arafat and the PLO. When Rabin heard about it, he continued the meetings, which culminated in the Oslo Accords (see "The Peace Process" chapter)—the ultimate land-for-peace appeasement deal.

## BENJAMIN NETANYAHU (1996–1999)

Benjamin Netanyahu was born in 1949, making him the first prime minister born after Israel became a nation. Educated in the U.S., he was the first prime minister who was not part of the old guard of *Haganah* and the *Irgun*.

He was, however, a unit team leader in the elite Special Forces unit of the IDF called the *Sayeret Matkal*, which means "General Staff Reconnaissance." The unit was used to counter terrorism, rescue hostages, and gather intelligence from behind enemy lines. It is most famous for Operation Thunderbolt, the mission that recovered a planeload of mostly Jewish hostages held by PLO terrorists at Entebbe airport in Uganda. Netanyahu's brother, Yoni, led that mission and was the only Israeli soldier who was killed.

In the unit, Netanyahu fought repeatedly against Syria to keep the Golan Heights in Israeli hands.

After his service in the IDF, Bibi (his nickname) initiated and organized a 1979 international conference against terrorism, which influenced world leaders, including future President George Bush Sr. and future Secretary of State George Schultz. Bibi served in several positions before becoming head of the Likud party in the *Knesset*.

In the 1996 election, he promised:

- Under his leadership, Israel "will never descend from the Golan."
- Israel would refuse to fulfill any part of a peace agreement until the Arabs kept theirs. Unless terrorism stopped and the PLO charter was rewritten to recognize Israel, no territory would be ceded. He insisted that giving land away would not guarantee peace, especially when it would compromise Israeli security. After all, the Syrians could shoot at Israelis from atop the Golan Heights!
- His campaign slogan was: "Netanyahu—making a safe peace."
- He said that a peace process would be okay, but he refused to ever give up the Golan Heights.
- He would encourage building in the Jewish settlements of the West Bank.
- He would never even discuss dividing Jerusalem.
- Once elected, Netanyahu appointed Ariel Sharon as his defense minister. Sharon was known for his insistence that the Arabs agree to all Israeli terms.

Once Netanyahu was in office, he returned Hebron to the Palestinians as part of a past agreement. Terrorism did not stop! The PLO charter remained unchanged!

In 1999, Daniel Pipes wrote an article in the *New Republic* magazine in which he revealed secret dealings between Netanyahu and King Assad of Syria. "Netanyahu had promised that under his leadership Israel would never descend from the Golan. In 1998, however, as I established in *The New Republic* and Bill Clinton just confirmed in his memoirs, Netanyahu changed his mind and planned to offer Damascus the entire Golan in return for a peace treaty."[27]

Why would Netanyahu be so blatantly two-faced? Was it ego? Was it trying to get elected or wanting to be known as the hero who won the peace? Could forces outside Israel be in control of the situation, forcing him to play ball? What role did U.S. pressure play?

The U.S., Israel, and the PLO held a summit at the Wye River Plantation in Maryland from October 16–23, 1998 (see "The Peace Process" chapter). For a week, Clinton, Netanyahu, and Arafat endured marathon talks with almost no sleep. The issues included Israel giving away land and releasing Palestinian prisoners, and the PLO changing the section in their charter that called for the destruction of Israel.

Netanyahu almost walked out amidst the pressure and the tension. Sharon was insisting that Israel not agree to give away any land, especially from the West Bank settlements. (As opposed to what Sharon did as prime minister in 2005!) The talks stalled.

Then President Clinton brought in King Hussein of Jordan, who was being treated in the U.S. for cancer. Weak and bald and almost at the end of his fight for life, the king gave an emotional speech, begging for peace, which was aired on televisions all over the world.

A weary, bleary-eyed, and visibly defeated Netanyahu ended up signing the Wye River Accords, whereby Israel released 199 Palestinian security prisoners on September 9, 1999, a day earlier than scheduled. Later in the day, Israel was to hand Palestinian leader Yasser Arafat the maps outlining the transfer of 7 percent of the West Bank (160 square miles) to Palestinian civil control as agreed in the new timetable for implementing the Wye agreement.

Israel also explicitly clarified that a section of the territory to be transferred to Palestinian civilian control would maintain the status of a nature reserve—in keeping with all the restrictions, reservations, and obligations set forth in the Wye River Memorandum. The Palestinians agreed to consider the change in their charter, but of course, it remained unchanged.

Netanyahu was swayed not just by King Hussein but by the false promises of President Clinton to release Jonathan Pollard (see my chapter on Pollard). Netanyahu leaked that promise to the press, and the U.S. vehemently denied it. Netanyahu was shamed into signing the agreement.

After the Wye meeting, the people of Israel voted Netanyahu out of office and elected Bibi's former commander in the Unit, Ehud Barak.

Netanyahu ran for reelection in 1999. In a televised debate with his former Defense Minister Yitzhak Mordechai, Netanyahu promised that he would never "give to Assad what Barak is willing to give to Assad." Mordechai challenged the candidate to dare repeat that statement while looking him in the eye. Netanyahu sat back speechless.

Bibi knew that Mordechai was there in 1998 when Netanyahu secretly promised the Golan Heights to Syria in exchange for almost nothing. The deal fell though, either because Netanyahu came to his senses or because Mordechai and Sharon would have none of it.

In 1998, however, Netanyahu once again planned to offer Damascus the entire Golan in return for a peace treaty.

In 2005, he apparently returned to his anti-land grant mode; Netanyahu resigned as finance minister in protest of Israel's planned pullout from the Gaza Strip.

## EHUD BARAK (1999–2001)

Just like his predecessor, Netanyahu, Ehud Barak was a military hero from the elite *Sayeret Matkal*. Better than that, Barak was its leader. No wonder he became the chief of staff of Israel's armed forces, the IDF. He held the highest rank in Israel, Lt. General.

Israel trusted that their top soldier would be able to deal decisively with their enemies!

In Barak's 1999 campaign, he promised:

- Jerusalem, united and under our rule forever, period.
- No return to the 1967 lines, period.
- There will not be a foreign army west of the Jordan.
- Most of the settlers will remain in settlement groups under our sovereignty.
- That the citizens could vote before any peace treaty with Syria would be ratified.

So what did Barak do at Camp David 2000 (see "The Peace Process" chapter)? Without any authorization from his government, Barak agreed to the U.S. Bridging Proposal to divide Jerusalem. He would have awarded East Jerusalem to the Palestinians! He also allowed them to build a tunnel under the Temple Mount, leading to the Al-Aqsa mosque. That tunnel destroyed many irreplaceable relics from temple days.

Israel had possession of the entire city of Jerusalem. Incredibly, Barak acted on his own, offering the city back to Israel's enemies. The world watched Israel being double-crossed by its own leader!

Luckily for Barak, Yasser Arafat turned him down! He was insisting that all his demands be met, including the right of return for Palestinian refugees. Barak did not agree to that.

The nation was not pleased by Barak's negotiating skills. He lost the 2001 election to Ariel Sharon by a landslide. People turned to Sharon, another war hero, to protect their country.

## ARIEL SHARON (2001–2006)

Sharon was a war hero, a hard-nosed general known for his no-nonsense defense of Israel's expanding borders. He fought in the military all his life, starting in 1942 in the *Haganah* at age fourteen. General Sharon was credited with Israel's victory in the 1973 Yom Kippur War. (See the chapter on "Miracles.")

A controversial figure, Sharon took the brunt of the blame for the 1982 massacre at the Sabra and Shatila refugee camps in Lebanon. No Israelis killed anyone; the Israeli army allowed the Lebanese Christian Phalangist militia to enter the camps, thinking that the militia was hunting for terrorist groups within the camp. Instead, they murdered 500–800 Palestinian civilians. An investigation found Sharon negligent for letting the militia in. Sharon resigned from his post as defense minister.

Campaigning for prime minister against Ehud Barak, Sharon promised he would defend the settlers of Judea, Samaria, and Gaza, and that he would help them build strong Jewish communities there. His promises resulted in a landslide victory.

People in Israel were relieved to have a strong, decisive leader who would stand up to the Arabs!

Running for reelection in 2003, Sharon defeated challenger Amram Mitzna, who favored "evacuating the settlements from Gaza." Sharon actually mocked Mitzna, warning that it "would bring the terrorism centers closer to [Israel's] population centers."

Sharon also declared, "A unilateral withdrawal is not a recipe for peace. It is a recipe for war."

So who became the architect of disengagement? Who insisted on using IDF soldiers to forcibly evict from Gaza the very settlers who voted for him and his promises to protect their homes?

Sharon was not finished with his disengaging, not even with the Hamas terrorists bragging about bringing tons of weapons into the newly Palestinian-ized Gaza. He planned to keep giving land away, first from the West Bank and then from Jerusalem!

In November 2005, Sharon told the Knesset that one of the goals of his new political party, Kadima, was to follow the U.S.-backed Road Map. The cornerstone of the Road Map is land for peace.

Before taking office, Sharon insisted that he would never negotiate with terrorists for the return of hostages. So who was it in February 2004 that released 429 Palestinian terrorists and other criminals? In exchange, Israel received one Israeli civilian and the corpses of three soldiers. Was this a deal?

As if God rewarded him according to his actions, Ariel Sharon was stricken with a debilitating stroke, resulting in a long coma. With the sudden end of his leadership, he was replaced by the even more concession-minded Ehud Olmert.

This part's history ends with Ariel Sharon. Ehud Olmert became prime minister in 2005. He will be discussed further in the chapters that follow.

# 6

# *Is the Bible the* Deed to Israel?

The Palestinians believe that Israel is a hostile aggressor illegally occupying their land. The Palestinian charter calls for the total destruction of Israel. The U.N., the European Union (E.U.), the news media, and many countries seem to agree that Israel has no right to be there (or anywhere!).

Israel maintains that it owns not just the land they have now, but much more. On what does Israel base their claim?

There are four methods of acquiring land:

1. Buy it.
2. Inherit it.
3. Receive it as a gift.
4. Conquer it.

When you buy land, you file a deed at the county clerk's office. When you inherit land, the deceased's will is read by an attorney, and then the deed is filed. If the land is a gift, you file your new deed. A conquering army sets up a government and establishes diplomatic relations with other countries. Those countries officially recognize the new government. That recognition acts like a deed.

In the Bible, it is written that God gave the land of Israel to the Israelites. Would that stand up in court today as a legal claim? Is the Bible the legal deed to the land of Israel? When Moses wrote down the Torah (Genesis through Deuteronomy), was he filing a legal property deed?

## THE BIBLICAL TRAIL OF OWNERSHIP

The biblical trail of ownership starts with Abram, before his name changed.

> *The LORD had said to Abram, "Leave your country,*
> *your people and your father's household and go*
> *to the land I will show you."*
> **GENESIS 12:1**

Abram went forth as God instructed. Upon arriving in Canaan:

> *The LORD appeared to Abram and said,*
> *"To your offspring I will give this land."*
> **GENESIS 12:7**

Abram's nephew Lot had so much livestock that he needed his own pastures. So Abram gave Lot his choice of property. Lot chose the plains of Sodom, leaving Abram with all the territory described here:

> *Abram lived in the land of Canaan, while Lot lived*
> *among the cities of the plain and pitched his tents near*
> *Sodom.... The LORD said to Abram after Lot had parted*
> *from him, "Lift up your eyes from where you are and look*
> *north and south, east and west. All the land that you see I*
> *will give to you and your offspring forever. I will make your*
> *offspring like the dust of the earth, so that if anyone could*
> *count the dust, then your offspring could be counted. Go,*

> *walk through the length and breadth of the land,*
> *for I am giving it to you."*
> GENESIS 13:12–17

To reassure Abram that he really owned all that land, the Lord made what is called the "Covenant of the Parts" with Abram. God formalized the land transaction by telling Abram to cut several animals in half and arrange the halves facing each other:

> *He also said to him, "I am the LORD, who brought you*
> *out of Ur of the Chaldeans to give you this land to take*
> *possession of it." But Abram said, "O Sovereign LORD,*
> *how can I know that I will gain possession of it?"*
> *When the sun had set and darkness had fallen,*
> *a smoking firepot with a blazing torch appeared and*
> *passed between the pieces. On that day the LORD*
> *made a covenant with Abram and said, "To your*
> *descendants I give this land, from the river of Egypt to*
> *the great river, the Euphrates, the land of the Kenites,*
> *Kenizzites, Kadmonites, Hittites, Perizzites, Rephaites,*
> *Amorites, Canaanites, Girgashites and Jebusites."*
> GENESIS 15:7–8, 17–21

The Torah also includes another comprehensive description of Abram's land grant in Deuteronomy:

> *"Break camp and advance into the hill country of the*
> *Amorites; go to all the neighboring peoples in the Arabah,*
> *in the mountains, in the western foothills, in the Negev and*
> *along the coast, to the land of the Canaanites and to Lebanon,*
> *as far as the great river, the Euphrates. See, I have given you*
> *this land. Go in and take possession of the land that the LORD*
> *swore he would give to your fathers—to Abraham, Isaac and*
> *Jacob—and to their descendants after them."*
> DEUTERONOMY 1:7–8

Notice the description of Israel's borders. Not only can the Bible be looked at as Israel's legal deed, it is also the survey map!

## LAND ACQUISITION

From Adam and Eve to Noah and the flood, the history of the Bible was passed down orally from father to son until Moses wrote it all down in the Torah. Noah knew it, and he taught it to his sons. Noah's son Shem educated the sons of many generations.

Most people don't realize that Shem was still alive during Abraham's lifetime. If you trace the lineage of Genesis 11:10–26, Shem was Abraham's great-great-great-great-great-great-great-grandfather! (That's seven greats.)

The genealogy from Adam onward was meticulously preserved. One reason was to demonstrate that Yeshua descended from Abraham through David. The other reason is to prove ownership of the land of Israel as it passed down through Abraham's offspring!

## ABRAHAM GETS THE DEED TO A FIELD IN HEBRON

When Sarah died, Abraham wanted to bury her in Hebron. He bought the burial site from a Hittite:

-----

*Ephron answered Abraham: "Listen to me, my lord;*
*the land is worth four hundred shekels of silver,*
*but what is that between me and you? Bury your dead."*
*Abraham agreed to Ephron's terms and weighed out for*
*him the price he had named in the hearing of the Hittites:*
*four hundred shekels of silver, according to the weight*
*current among the merchants. So Ephron's field in Machpelah*
*near Mamre—both the field and the cave in it, and all the*
*trees within the borders of the field—was deeded to Abraham*
*as his property in the presence of all the Hittites who had*
*come to the gate of the city. Afterward Abraham buried his*
*wife Sarah in the cave in the field of Machpelah near Mamre*
*(which is at Hebron) in the land of Canaan. So the field and*

> *the cave in it were deeded to Abraham*
> *by the Hittites as a burial site.*
> GENESIS 23:14–20

Did Abraham file a paper deed with the Hebron county clerk? No, but there were other people present at the transaction. It later appeared on paper in the Torah.

## ISAAC AND ISHMAEL: WHO IS THE LEGAL HEIR?

Ishmael was Abraham's firstborn son. Normally, Abraham's inheritance would have gone to him, but Ishmael was not the son whom God had promised. He was the fruit of Sarah and Abraham's impatience. Ishmael was not the legitimate son!

Once Isaac, the legal heir, was born, Sarah moved to protect his birthright:

> *The child grew and was weaned, and on the day Isaac*
> *was weaned Abraham held a great feast. But Sarah saw that*
> *the son whom Hagar the Egyptian had borne to Abraham*
> *was mocking, and she said to Abraham, "Get rid of that*
> *slave woman and her son, for that slave woman's son will*
> *never share in the inheritance with my son Isaac." The matter*
> *distressed Abraham greatly because it concerned his son.*
> *But God said to him, "Do not be so distressed about the*
> *boy and your maidservant. Listen to whatever Sarah tells*
> *you, because it is through Isaac that your offspring will be*
> *reckoned. I will make the son of the maidservant into*
> *a nation also, because he is your offspring."*
> GENESIS 21:8–13

Abraham sent Hagar and Ishmael off into the desert. Ishmael stayed in touch with Abraham. He was there for his father's burial alongside Sarah:

> *His sons Isaac and Ishmael buried him in the cave of*
> *Machpelah near Mamre.*
> GENESIS 25:9

But Abraham cut Ishmael out of his will:

> *Abraham left everything he owned to Isaac.*
> GENESIS 25:5

Soon after Abraham's death, the Lord confirmed to Isaac that he was the heir to the Promised Land. Isaac sought refuge from the famine in Gerar, home of the Philistine kings. God told Isaac that he would own "all of these lands," which would include all the lands of the Philistines:

> *Now there was a famine in the land—besides the earlier famine of Abraham's time—and Isaac went to Abimelech king of the Philistines in Gerar. The LORD appeared to Isaac and said, "Do not go down to Egypt; live in the land where I tell you to live. Stay in this land for a while, and I will be with you and will bless you. For to you and your descendants I will give all these lands and will confirm the oath I swore to your father Abraham. I will make your descendants as numerous as the stars in the sky and will give them all these lands, and through your offspring all nations on earth will be blessed..."*
> GENESIS 26:1–4

All of the Jewish people are Isaac's descendants. The Arabs are all descendants of Ishmael. According to the Bible, Jewish people are the heirs to Israel. The Arab people are not.

## JOSHUA: A SURVEY MAP FOR EACH TRIBE!

In the book of Joshua, the Lord went into much detail about the borders of the Promised Land, giving us a survey map of each tribe's land, from Reuben to Ephraim. Many of the locations are unknown to us today, but we can get a good idea of how extensive the nation of Israel is supposed to be.

Joshua and his army had to fight to wrest these territories from the "ites" who inhabited them. Joshua 12 records the kings who were defeated by Israel under Joshua. The list includes the king of Hebron and the king of Jerusalem: That means that Hebron and Jerusalem and all the other places became the legal property of Israel.

*These are the kings of the land that Joshua and the Israelites conquered on the west side of the Jordan...the king of Jerusalem one, the king of Hebron one.*
JOSHUA 12:7, 10

There is one more requirement for land ownership: You have to take possession of it. In Joshua 21, all the tribes had done that:

*So the LORD gave Israel all the land he had sworn to give their forefathers, and they took possession of it and settled there.*
JOSHUA 21:43

## JERUSALEM: OWNERSHIP BY CONQUEST

By the time of King David, the Jebusites had regained strength in Jerusalem. David had to conquer the city from them:

*David captured the fortress of Zion, the City of David...
David then took up residence in the fortress and
called it the City of David.*
2 SAMUEL 5:7, 9

Jerusalem became more than the capital city of Israel. It was the holy city where God's presence dwelt in the Holy of Holies, inside the temple.

Herod's Temple was destroyed in A.D. 70, and the Jewish people were scattered. Although many nations ruled over it, Jerusalem was a barren wasteland for almost 2,000 years. Jerusalem has been back in Jewish hands since 1967, and it is now thriving.

The Palestinians want it as their capital, claiming that it is the holy city of the Koran. What is the truth? If they really wanted their capital there, they could have established it centuries ago. When England occupied Jerusalem, the Arab citizens did not try to overthrow England and set up a capital.

The most important real estate in the world today, Jerusalem remains at the center of world conflict. It has been claimed by everyone from the Arabs to the Vatican. The late Pope John Paul II wanted to make Jerusalem an international city, not owned by any one country. The peace process has been aiming at the surrender of Jerusalem. What a frightening proposition! God calls Jerusalem the "apple of His eye" and warns us not to mess with her:

> *Then I looked up—and there before me was a man*
> *with a measuring line in his hand! I asked, "Where are*
> *you going?" He answered me, "To measure Jerusalem, to*
> *find out how wide and how long it is.... And I myself will be a*
> *wall of fire around it," declares the LORD, "and I will be*
> *its glory within....for whoever touches you touches the*
> *apple of his eye—I will surely raise my hand against them*
> *so that their slaves will plunder them."*
> ZECHARIAH 2:1–2, 5, 8–9

Tough words from God! Is it proof that Israel owns Jerusalem? Who would challenge God on it?

## MOUNT MORIAH: THE *AKEIDAH*

In Genesis 22, God gave Abraham a heart-wrenching command: Go to the top of Mount Moriah and put his son Isaac to death as a sacrifice. The story is called the *Akeidah* by orthodox Jews. That morning, father and son set out for their trip:

> *When they reached the place God had told him about,*
> *Abraham built an altar there and arranged the wood*
> *on it. He bound his son Isaac and laid him on the altar,*
> *on top of the wood.*
> GENESIS 22:9

For the first time, an altar was built on top of Mount Moriah. Abraham was not making an offering for sin; his obedience was being tested. Before Abraham could thrust the knife into Isaac, the Angel of the

Lord stopped him. There in the thicket was a ram, its horns stuck in the branches. Abraham sacrificed the ram instead of Isaac. Abraham called the mountaintop *Yahweh Yireh*, which is known in English as *Jehovah Jireh* (God sees and provides):

> *So Abraham called that place The LORD Will Provide.*
> *And to this day it is said, "On the mountain of*
> *the LORD it will be provided."*
> GENESIS 22:14

Abraham's obedience merited a blessing from the angel:

> *"I will surely bless you and make your descendants*
> *as numerous as the stars in the sky and as the sand*
> *on the seashore. Your descendants will take*
> *possession of the cities of their enemies."*
> GENESIS 22:17

One of those cities was Jerusalem. Mount Moriah rises up in the middle of Jerusalem. It is known as the Temple Mount.

## THE THRESHING FLOOR

This is the historical account of how King David acquired the threshing floor, the site of the Temple Mount.

In 2 Samuel 24:1–17, God told David not to count his army, but David disobeyed and took a census. God punished the army with a plague. David had to build an altar in order to offer a sacrifice to atone for his sin and stop the plague.

> *On that day Gad went to David and said to him,*
> *"Go up and build an altar to the LORD on the threshing*
> *floor of Araunah the Jebusite." So David went up,*
> *as the LORD had commanded through Gad.*
> 2 SAMUEL 24:18–19

God sent David to the same place where Abraham built his altar. Araunah's threshing floor was on the top of Mount Moriah. Araunah offered to give David the property and the animals to use for sacrifice. David refused.

> *But the king replied to Araunah, "No, I insist on paying*
> *you for it. I will not sacrifice to the LORD my God burnt*
> *offerings that cost me nothing." So David bought the threshing*
> *floor and the oxen and paid fifty shekels of silver for them.*
>
> 2 SAMUEL 24:24

David bought the Temple Mount from Araunah the Jebusite. The deed is recorded in 2 Samuel 24.

> *"O king, Araunah gives all this to the king."*
>
> 2 SAMUEL 24:23

The verse is stated differently in other translations. According to the King James Version, it reads, "All these things did Araunah, a king, give unto the king." Young's Literal Translation says, "The whole hath Araunah given, [as] a king to a king." And the Masoretic text reads, "All this did the king give unto the king."

According to these translations, Araunah was the Jebusite king. He may have been the king of all Jerusalem! Clearly, he was not just a farmer threshing his grain. His property was on top of the mountain in the center of the city. As king, he had the authority to give or sell this place to King David.

Araunah was part of the remnant of the Jebusites. Later, in 2 Chronicles 8, David's son Solomon made the Jebusites become slaves:

> *All the people left from the Hittites, Amorites, Perizzites,*
> *Hivites and Jebusites (these peoples were not Israelites),*
> *that is, their descendants remaining in the land, whom the*
> *Israelites had not destroyed—these Solomon conscripted*
> *for his slave labor force, as it is to this day.*
>
> 2 CHRONICLES 8:7–8

First Chronicles 21 tells the story in greater detail, with most translations using the name Ornan instead of Araunah.

*Araunah said to David, "Let my lord the king take
whatever pleases him and offer it up. Here are oxen
for the burnt offering, and here are threshing
sledges and ox yokes for the wood.*

2 Samuel 24:22

*And Ornan said unto David, Take it to thee, and let my lord
the king do that which is good in his eyes: lo, I give thee the
oxen also for burnt offerings, and the threshing instruments
for wood, and the wheat for the meat offering; I give it all.*

1 Chronicles 21:23 kjv

*Strong's Concordance* defines *Ornan* or *Araunah* as "a pine tree; a fir or ash. It is a very strong tree from which idols were carved; makes a whirring sound when shaken by the wind; tremulous; nervous shaking (sounds like threshing!). He was also a man of Jebus which was the early name for Jerusalem."

## WHO WERE THE JEBUSITES?

According to *Strong's Concordance, Jebus* means "a place trodden down, as a threshing floor." Jebus was Noah's grandson. Ham was his father. When Ham pointed out his father's nakedness in Genesis 9:22, Noah cursed Ham's descendants through Canaan. He said that they would be slaves forever. That came to pass under Solomon.

A *threshing floor* is defined as "a smooth, level place."

The smooth, trodden-down threshing floor was on Mount Moriah, site of the *Ameidah*. The threshing floor on Mount Moriah became the site of the temple, known as the Temple Mount. It was bought and paid for by the king of Israel at the command of Yahweh. Solomon built the great temple right on that spot.

Today the Islamic mosque called the Dome of the Rock is on the Temple Mount. Jews are not even allowed to go up there. They can only stand at the bottom of the Western Wall, the sole remnant of the temple on Mount Moriah.

# NEHEMIAH 9

After Judah had been in exile in Babylon for 70 years, Ezra and Nehemiah returned to Jerusalem to rebuild the temple as well as the wall around the city. It was time to reclaim Jewish ownership of the land. After the temple was rebuilt, the Levites brought out the Torah and read it to everyone. The Levites summarized much of the land allotment:

*"You are the LORD God, who chose Abram and brought him out of Ur of the Chaldeans and named him Abraham. You found his heart faithful to you, and you made a* covenant with him to give to his descendants the land *of the Canaanites, Hittites, Amorites, Perizzites, Jebusites and Girgashites. You have kept your promise because you are righteous."*
NEHEMIAH 9:7–8 (EMPHASIS ADDED, MINE)

*You gave them kingdoms and nations, allotting to them even the remotest frontiers. They took over the country of Sihon king of Heshbon and the country of Og king of Bashan. You made their sons as numerous as the stars in the sky, and you brought them into the land that you told their fathers to enter and possess. Their sons went in and took possession of the land. You subdued before them the Canaanites, who lived in the land; you handed the Canaanites over to them, along with their kings and the peoples of the land, to deal with them as they pleased. They captured fortified cities and fertile land; they took possession of houses filled with all kinds of good things, wells already dug, vineyards, olive groves and fruit trees in abundance.*
NEHEMIAH 9:22–25

# WHO HAD JERUSALEM?

One after the other, armies rose up to conquer the world. The biggest prize was Jerusalem. The holy city was occupied by all these nations and their leaders:

1800 B.C.   The Jebusites (Araunah)

993 B.C.   Israel (King David)

606–586 B.C.   Babylonians (King Nebuchadnezzar)

537 B.C.   Persia (King Cyrus)

332 B.C.   Greece: Hellenistic domination (Alexander the Great)

313 B.C.   Egypt (Ptolemy I)

175–165 B.C.   Seleucids; Syrian/Greeks (Antiochus Epiphanes)

165 B.C.   Israel; the Maccabees recapture Jerusalem (Hasmoneans; Judas Maccabee)

63 B.C.   Rome (Pompey)

324   Byzantine Empire

614   Persian (General Shahrbaraz)

629   Byzantine Empire (Heraclius)

638   Muslim Arabs (Caliph Umar)

1099   The Crusades

1190   Kurdish Muslims (Saladdin)

1244   Khwarezmian Tatars (modern Uzbekistan)

1247   Egypt

1259   Mongols (Genghis Khan)

1260   Mamelukes (slave soldiers of the caliphs and Ottomans)

1517   Ottoman Empire: Turks (Sultan Selim)

1831   Egypt (Sultan Mehmet Ali)

1838   Great Britain

1840   The Ottoman Turks

1917   Great Britain (General Allenby)

1948   The Jewish State of Israel

Israel was an arid, unfertile desert for centuries. It only bloomed under Jewish control.

In 1922, the League of Nations appointed England to rule over Israel. They called it Palestine instead of Israel as an insult to the Jews. The name Palestine was based on the Philistines, the nemesis of ancient Israel. *Strong's Concordance* defines *Philistines* as "immigrants and sojourners." What an affront to the Jews, who had endured so much suffering and wandering and were finally coming home!

There never was a people group called the Palestinians. British-occupied Palestine was populated by Arabs, Christians, and Jews as well as people from many nations. All of them were called Palestinians because they lived there.

Israel became a nation in May 1948. As the surrounding Arab countries prepared to attack, they called on Arab citizens in Israel to leave so the Arabs could drive all the Jews into the sea. When they failed to do that, they placed their displaced brethren into refugee camps. Jordan should have accepted them as citizens, since many of them came from Jordan's new territories. Instead they used the refugees to evoke sympathy from the world. The Palestinians still demand an independent state, but they never were a distinct group of people!

In Abraham's day, there were no Palestinians living in Canaan! All of the original people groups became extinct. None of them are around to lay claim to the land today. The Palestinians did not descend from the Jebusites!

## CONCLUSION

Once again, you can get land four ways:
1. Buy it.
2. Inherit it.
3. Receive it as a gift.
4. Conquer it.

Jerusalem, the Temple Mount, and all of Israel belong to the Jewish people because:
1. Abraham bought the field. David bought the threshing floor.
2. The land was inherited by the descendants of Abraham, through Isaac.
3. God gave the land to Israel as a gift.
4. Israel's armies conquered the inhabitants.

Wait! There's one more way! In *Eretz Israel*, there is one more way to get property. Leviticus 25:8–34 speaks of the Year of Jubilee. Every fiftieth year is a Jubilee year in Israel. At the Jubilee year, all property reverts to its original owner among the tribes of Israel!

> *Consecrate the fiftieth year and proclaim liberty throughout the land to all its inhabitants. It shall be a jubilee for you; each one of you is to return to his family property and each to his own clan.... In this Year of Jubilee everyone is to return to his own property.*
> LEVITICUS 25:10, 13

No matter who buys, claims, or grabs a single inch of property in Israel, the original family is supposed to get it back at Jubilee. All property should revert to the families that owned it back in Joshua's day!

The problem is only Jewish people honor the Bible's authority to grant ownership of property. In fact, most people do not recognize any authority in God's Word.

In the U.S., if a family moved into your house without your permission (squatting), you would call the sheriff to come and evict them. That's because U.S. law is accepted as the authority to enforce U.S. land rights.

How can Israel get the rest of the world to respect its law, the Torah? That can only be done with God's help! If the world will not respect Israel's ownership of the land, God will help them defend it every time! It can't hurt to have the prayers of God's people backing up the Law, like a posse.

Anyone who believes that the Bible is the actual Word of God has to believe that the Jewish people own the land of Israel. For those who don't believe it, it doesn't matter. It is still true!

# 7

# *Israel as the* Time Clock

There is no spiritual void. As the history of Israel unfolds, the rest of the world is affected one way or the other. God's body of believers, the Church, gets blessed or cursed by how they have treated Israel. When Israel is scattered, the Church suffers. When Israel is restored, mighty moves of the Holy Spirit break out. There is no coincidence in the kingdom of God!

> *The LORD said to Abram, "Leave your country, your people and your father's household and go into the land I will show you. I will make you a great nation and I will bless you; I will make your name great, and you will be a blessing. I will bless those who bless you, and whoever curses you I will curse; and all peoples on earth will be blessed through you."*
> GENESIS 12:1–3

> *"But they will say, 'As surely as the LORD lives, who
> brought the descendants of Israel out of the land of the north
> and out of all the countries where he had banished them.'
> Then they will live in their own land."*
> JEREMIAH 23:8

> *Go, proclaim this message toward the north: "Return, faithless
> Israel," declares the LORD, "I will frown on you no longer, for I
> am merciful," declares the LORD, "I will not be angry forever."*
> JEREMIAH 3:12

> *"Do not be afraid, for I am with you; I will bring your
> children from the east and gather you from the west.
> I will say to the north, 'Give them up!' and to the south,
> 'Do not hold them back!' Bring my sons from afar and my
> daughters from the ends of the earth."*
> ISAIAH 43:5–6

## ISRAEL AS A TIME CLOCK

Let's take a look at Israel as a time clock to see how events in Israel manifest in the Church.

*A.D. 70*

Israel suffers persecution. The temple is destroyed by Romans, and the Jews are persecuted, exiled, and scattered. Christians experience a similar oppression.

*100–1400s*

In Israel, the Jews are still persecuted, exiled, and scattered, while individual freedom declines as the Catholic Church seizes more and more power over people. Europe enters the Dark Ages.

*1490s*

In Europe, the Catholic Church begins the Inquisition to force Jews to convert. They suffer torture or death in the name of Jesus. Jews are exiled from Spain and Portugal and scattered throughout the world. Thus a big Jewish influx begins. Jews arrive into the New World.

## 1500s

In Europe, Jewish persecution and genocide intensify as the Inquisition continues. The Reformation of the Church begins as Martin Luther returns the Word of God to the people, but he becomes very anti-Semitic.

## 1800s

In Europe, Theodore Hertzl leads the Zionism movement as Jews begin returning to the land of Israel. Jewish pioneers settle in the wilderness—in desert and swamps—in Palestine. In Europe and the U.S., holiness revivals begin in the Christian Church, along with a great rise in cults.

The first Jewish community, Petah Tikvah (Door of Hope), is built outside of Jerusalem without walls. Ezekiel 38:11 is beginning to be fulfilled: "You will say, 'I will invade a land of unwalled villages; I will attack a peaceful and unsuspecting people—all of them living without walls and without gates and bars.'"

Interestingly, the latter rain had ceased falling on the land, but when the Jewish people began to return, it again started.[28]

During this time, the Lord was at work with a wonderful outpouring of His love. It started in New York City with a small group of people praying in the Dutch North Church and quickly spread as a massive Holy Spirit revival throughout America and then the world. It was a true Latter Rain move of God that coincided with His children being called back to the Land of Promise.[29]

Holiness revivals begin in the Church, healing houses were raised up by Charles Cullis and healing ministries such as those of A. B. Simpson, Maria B. Woodworth-Etter, John Alexander Dowie, and others.[30]

## Early 1900s

Zionist pioneers continue to settle in the land, while Zionist leaders consider and reject Britain's offer to set up their nation in the African country of Uganda. In America, Pentecostal revival begins at Azusa Street in Los Angeles. This revival grew into the Pentecostal movement and led to the formation of the Assemblies of God. In 1945, this church splits along racial lines, with the black community founding the Church of God in Christ and the United Pentecostal Church.

## 1948

Israel becomes a nation. In November 1947, the U.N. voted in favor of the partition of Palestine, proposing the creation of a Jewish state, an Arab state, and a U.N.-administered Jerusalem. This partition was accepted by Zionist leaders, but rejected by Arab leaders, resulting in the 1947–1948 Civil War in Mandatory Palestine. Israel declared independence on May 14, 1948, and neighboring Arab states attacked the next day.

In the U.S., the Latter Rain Revival and large healing ministries were born and quickly spread throughout Canada and around the world. Oral Roberts, Jack Coe, Kathryn Kuhlman, A. A. Allen, and others led the way.

## 1967

The Six-Day War between Israel and its neighboring states of Egypt, Jordan, and Syria took place on June 5–10. At the war's end, Israel had gained control of the Sinai Peninsula, the Gaza Strip, the West Bank, East Jerusalem, and the Golan Heights. The war results in Israel reclaiming Jerusalem.

In the U.S., the Jesus Movement starts in Haight-Ashbury, San Francisco, and spreads throughout the world. At the same time in the same place, Satan raises up the hippie movement, spreading throughout the world.

## 1970s

Israel miraculously wins the Yom Kippur War in 1973.

The Jesus Movement grows among baby boomers, spreading primarily through North America and Europe. In California, the Lord raises up the beginnings of the Messianic movement with leaders such as Marty Chernoff. Major teaching ministries begin, e.g. Kenneth Hagin, Kenneth Copeland, and others. Future leaders come from this move of God, such as Rick Joyner, Greg Laurie, and many more.

*1980s*

The world's attention is on the Middle East and the peace process in Israel.

In the Church the Charismatic Movement brings the increase of spiritual gifts, ministries, charismatic Catholics, and the growth of churches into megachurches.

*1990s*

More Middle East Peace initiatives threaten Israel.

The move of God continues with a series of revivals at Toronto, Pensacola, Smithton, etc.

*The End Times*

Daniel wrote about a seven-year covenant with the antichrist in Israel that lasts for three-and-a-half years and leads to the Abomination of Desolation.

---

*And he shall confirm the covenant with many for one week:*
*and in the midst of the week he shall cause the*
*sacrifice and the oblation to cease, and for the*
*overspreading of abominations he shall make it desolate,*
*even until the consummation, and that determined*
*shall be poured upon the desolate.*
DANIEL 9:27 JVC

---

Jacob's troubles start; Jerusalem is surrounded by armies; the world's armies gather. It is already described by Jeremiah and Luke.

---

*How awful that day will be! None will be like it. It will be a*
*time of trouble for Jacob, but he will be saved out of it.*
JEREMIAH 30:7

*When you see Jerusalem being surrounded by armies,*
*you will know that its desolation is near.*
LUKE 21:20

---

Satan is cast down! Yeshua comes! All Israel will be saved! He rules with all the saints for 1,000 years! The apostle Paul stated:

---

*And so all Israel shall be saved: as it is written:*
*"The deliverer will come from Zion; he will turn*
*godlessness away from Jacob."*
ROMANS 11:26

---

God begins to pour out His glory and power in various churches in America through miraculous healing, deep revelations of the Father's love, and the fire of God falling very powerfully. See a restoration of the mighty manifestations of the reality of God as in the book of Acts.

# 8

# *Israel's* Wars

Since Israel became a nation in 1948, it has had to defend itself in the following wars:

## 1948: THE ARAB-ISRAELI WAR

This was also called the Independence War or the War of Liberation. Immediately after the British pullout and declaration of statehood, the surrounding Arab nations attacked Israel. Their goal was to push all the Jews into the sea. Outnumbered a hundred to one, Israel defeated the Arabs and acquired more land.

## 1956: THE SUEZ WAR

This was also called Operation Kadesh. Returning to government, Ben-Gurion collaborated with the British and French to plan the 1956 Sinai War in which Israel stormed the Sinai Peninsula in retaliation for raids by Egypt. This gave the British and French forces a pretext to intervene in order to secure the Suez Canal after Egypt's President Gamal Abdel Nasser had announced its nationalization. Intervention by the U.S. and the U.N. forced the British, French, and Israelis to back down.[31]

## 1967: THE SIX-DAY WAR

In 1967, Egypt, Syria, and Jordan ganged up against Israel. It started with Egypt's ships blockading the Strait of Tiran—an important passageway for Israel's shipping. Within six days, Israel had taken more land than they had started with as a nation and received the victory on all fronts.

## 1970: THE WAR OF ATTRITION

This war was fought between Israel and Egypt from 1967–1970. It was initiated by Egypt as a way to force Israel to negotiate on favorable terms the return of the Sinai Peninsula, which had been captured by Israel in the 1967 Six-Day War. However, this objective was not realized, and instead the hostilities ended with a cease-fire signed between the countries in 1970 with frontiers remaining in the same place as when the war began, with no real commitment to serious peace negotiations.

## 1973: THE YOM KIPPUR WAR

In October 1973, Egypt and Syria launched a surprise attack against Israel on the holiest day of the Jewish calendar: Yom Kippur, the Day of Atonement. Knowing that Israel could not mobilize for defense with everything closed, including television and radio, they attacked on two fronts. Egypt crossed the Suez Canal to reclaim the Sinai Peninsula, while Syria attacked the Golan Heights. These territories had been won by Israel in the 1967 Six-Day War. Israel at the time was caught completely off-guard, despite the warning signs, and yet was able to recover and miraculously have success.

## 1982: THE LEBANON WAR

This war, also called Operation Peace for Galilee, began on June 6, 1982, when the Israel Defense Forces (IDF) invaded southern Lebanon.

The government of Israel decided to launch the military operation after the assassination attempt against Israel's ambassador to the United Kingdom, Shlomo Argov, by the Abu Nidal Organization, a mercenary organization opposed to the PLO.

After attacking the PLO, as well as Syrian leftist and Muslim Lebanese forces, Israel occupied southern Lebanon and eventually surrounded the PLO and elements of the Syrian army. Surrounded in west Beirut and subjected to heavy bombardment, they negotiated passage from Lebanon with the aid of Special Envoy Philip Habib and the protection of international peacekeepers.

## 1987–1993: THE FIRST INTIFADA

It was a Palestinian uprising against Israeli occupation in the Palestinian Territories. It started in the Jabalia refugee camp and quickly spread throughout Gaza, the West Bank, and East Jerusalem.

Palestinian actions primarily included civil disobedience and resistance movement. In addition to general strikes, boycotts on Israeli products, refusal to pay taxes, graffiti, and barricades, Palestinian demonstrations that included stone-throwing by youths against the Israel Defense Forces (IDF) defined the violence for many. The violence was directed at both Israeli soldiers and civilians.

Violence inside Palestine was also a prominent feature of the Intifada, with widespread executions of alleged Israeli collaborators. Over the course of the first intifada, an estimated 1,100 Palestinians were killed by Israeli forces, and 164 Israelis were killed by Palestinians. In addition, an estimated 1,000 Palestinians were killed by Palestinians as alleged collaborators, although fewer than half had any proven contact with the Israeli authorities.

## 1990/1: THE PERSIAN GULF

It was the response to Iraq's President Saddam Hussein's aggression. He had invaded Kuwait to acquire its rich oil fields. When he ignored the U.S. ultimatum to withdraw from Kuwait, the U.S. and other allies attacked Iraq with computer precision air strikes.

Hussein used the war as an excuse to attack Israel with his Scud missiles. Scuds are tactical ballistic missiles developed by the Soviet Union during the Cold War. The U.S. put tremendous pressure on Israel not to retaliate. Israel complied with America's request and watched and waited, though with a warrior's heart, this was difficult. Israel was the target of 39 of Hussein's Scuds, and he even threatened to launch chemical and biological weapons through the Scuds. The Jews were terrified because of what they had endured during the Holocaust.

I was at the White House ceremony in 1993 when the U.S. pressured Yitzhak Rabin to sign a peace accord with the infamous terrorist Yasser Arafat. I was sickened to see senators standing in line to get Arafat's autograph. A former Speaker of the House said to me, "I used to not like that fellow, but after his charming speech, I find him very delightful." Jesse Jackson smugly said, "The Jews need to follow the Golden Rule and give the Palestinians their state."

Yasser Arafat had no intention of ever making peace with Israel. It was never about having a state; it was about destroying a state: Israel.[32]

## 2000: AL-AQSA INTIFADA

Code named Ebb and Tide events by the Israeli Defense Forces, this is also named the Second Intifada—a wave of violence and political conflict that began in 2000 between Israel and the Palestinians.

Starting as early as September 13, 2000, members of Palestinian leader Yasser Arafat's Fatah movement carried out a number of attacks on Israeli military and civilian targets, in violation of Oslo Accords. In addition, the Israeli agency Palestinian Media Watch states that the Palestinian official television broadcasts became increasingly militant during the summer of 2000, as Camp David negotiations faltered. On September 27, the new Intifada claimed its first Israeli victim, the military officer Sgt. David Biri.

Israel claims that the Intifada was planned in advance by the Palestinian Authority leadership and executed in response to the failure of the Camp David 2000 Summit per statements made by Yasser Arafat, President of the Palestinian Authority.

9
___

# *Miracles—*
# Old and New

As children we were taught all the miracle stories in the Old Testament. Again and again, God saved the people of Israel by intervening in supernatural, spectacular ways. To list just a few miracles from the book of Exodus, God spoke to Moses with an audible voice from a burning bush that was not consumed; God sent plagues on the Egyptians to get Pharaoh to let them go; God parted the Red Sea so the Israelites could escape Pharaoh's chariots; God poured out water from a rock; and everybody's shoes lasted for 40 years!

Moses' successor, Joshua, needed a miracle to win the battle against the five Amorite kings (Joshua 10). He prayed for the sun to stand still to give him more time to defeat them. God answered Joshua's prayer. The sun kept shining all night.

In 2 Chronicles 20, Israel was about to be attacked by Moab and Ammon. King Jehoshaphat went before the Lord to pray for help. God told the king to send the Levite worship musicians into battle ahead of the armies. The Levites marched out and sang, "Give thanks to the LORD, for his love endures forever" (v. 21). The Lord sent confusion into the enemy camp. They turned on one another until every one of them was dead.

In December, we celebrate *Chanukah*, the Festival of Lights. The story appears in the Apocrypha, the book of the history between the Old and New Testaments. Although it is not in the Bible, Chanukah is based on the miracle of the victory by the small band of Maccabees over the mighty Syrian and Greek army that occupied Israel. The *menorah* reminds us that when the priests took back the temple, they only had one night's oil for the lamp stand, but it burned for the eight days and nights that it took to produce and consecrate new oil. While there is some debate as to the veracity of the eight-night oil story, the defeat of the occupying army was completely miraculous.

During the occupation of the Syrian-Greeks, Jewish children would play with a spinning top called a *draidel*, so they would not be caught studying their Bibles. The four Hebrew letters on the sides of the draidel are the first letters in the words: "A great miracle happened here!"

With folded arms and frowns, many modern Bible scholars insist that miracles are not for today. They say miracles were needed during biblical times, but not now. Let's take a look at the facts to see if they are right.

## MIRACLE: ISRAEL REBORN

After centuries of neglect, Israel had become a barren wasteland of desert and swamps. In the late 1800s and early 1900s, the Zionist pioneers slowly turned it back into the land of milk and honey that it was in Bible days. In the twentieth century, Israel was reborn with signs, wonders, and miracles!

On May 14, 1948, the U.N. declared that Israel was an independent nation. After 2,000 years of dispersion throughout the world, living in countries that hated them, threw them out, and killed them, the Jewish people finally had a home. All the Bible prophecies about restoring the Jews to the Promised Land came true in a day!

*Though you search for your enemies, you will not find them.
Those who wage war against you will be nothing at all. For I
am the LORD, your God, who takes hold of your right hand
and says to you, Do not fear; I will help you.*
ISAIAH 41:12–13

*Who has ever heard of such a thing? Who has ever seen such
things? Can a country be born in a day or a nation be brought
forth in a moment? Yet no sooner is Zion in labor than she
gives birth to her children.*
ISAIAH 66:8

## MIRACLE: THE HEBREW LANGUAGE

In the Diaspora, the dispersion among the nations, Jewish people spoke the languages of the countries they lived in. Hebrew was used only for prayers and reading scripture in synagogue.

David Ben-Gurion turned to the Bible in establishing this land of Israel. As a young man, David Ben-Gurion started a Hebrew club with his friends. As they started speaking to one another in Hebrew, God helped them restore their ancient language. At the time of this language being established, there were over 80 different people groups speaking their own tongues. An early pioneer in Israel, Eliezer Ben-Yehuda revived Hebrew as a language for speaking and writing. Hebrew had been forgotten for 2,000 years; today it is Israel's national language!

Following clues in the Bible concerning copper and iron, mines were discovered. One mining engineer observed that as they did their excavations they came upon ancient Israeli furnaces for extracting copper ore.

Archaeologists discovered the presence of more than 70 ancient settlement sites, each with its own well. New settlements from Dan to Beersheba have risen right beside ancient wells that are being used today for water. In the Bible, it says Abraham planted a tamarisk tree in Beersheba, so two million were planted, and it is the only tree that can survive the arid region.

# 1948 WAR

Immediately after the British pullout and declaration of statehood, the surrounding Arab nations attacked Israel. Their goal was to push all the Jews into the sea. Outnumbered a hundred to one, Israel defeated the Arabs and acquired more land.

How was this victory possible? Who caused so many miracles to establish the new nation and enable them to defend themselves? There is only one explanation: God moves in a supernatural way to save His chosen people!

## Two Ancient Cannons

Before their withdrawal, the British had confiscated all weapons from the Israelis. A Syrian column of 200 armored vehicles and 45 tanks advanced toward Degana—Israel's oldest *kibbutz* or cooperative farming community. Like all *kibbutzim*, Degana was filled with un-armed and helpless men, women, and lots of children.

The only weapons remaining in Israel were four howitzer cannons from the Franco-Prussian War of 1870. Two of them were rushed to Degana. Lt. Col. Moshe Dayan (the famous soldier with the eye patch) quickly reassembled the guns. Just as the enemy began to enter the property, the old howitzers hit and destroyed the first Syrian tank! The Syrians thought the Israelis had amassed an arsenal of powerful weapons. They did a quick about-face and ran away! Degana was saved by two ancient cannons! Or were they saved by the arm of the Lord?

## The Flaming Drums

At Safed near the Sea of Galilee, small units of Israelis were struggling to hold off thousands of Arabs. Suddenly there was a severe thunderstorm. The Israelis poured their remaining gasoline over 50 empty barrels, set them on fire, and rolled them down the hill. The flaming barrels combined with the crashing of the hollow drums against the rocks and the storm's thunder and wind gave the Arabs the illusion of a dreadful secret weapon. They turned and fled!

## The Forgotten Road

The Egyptians were attacking Israeli settlements in the Negev while their armored columns sped north. The Israelis read in the Bible about an ancient forgotten road that went almost to the camp of the Egyptian army. Israeli bulldozers quickly cleared the road. In the dark, they snuck up on the Egyptians with armored vehicles and supply trucks. The surprise attack defeated the Egyptians. The war ended 14 days later.

## The Impersonators

Looking again in the Bible, the Israelis were inspired by Gideon's army of 300 men. Gideon's men made so much noise that the enemy armies got confused and killed one another.

> The LORD said to Gideon, "With the three hundred men that lapped I will save you and give the Midianites into your hands. Let all the other men go, each to his own place."
> JUDGES 7:7

At the airport at Lydda in Israel, 7,000 Arab troops were ready to attack. Sixteen Israelis dressed as Arabs snuck into Lydda. They made such a commotion during the night that the Arabs got confused and fired on one another, then fled back across the border!

There were several battles in the *Tenach* that were won by the enemy getting confused and killing one another. Was it plain luck, or did God repeat the biblical pattern?

## The Wrong Road

Twenty-four Israeli armored vehicles were headed to a kibbutz that was under siege. They took a wrong turn and unknowingly crossed the border into Lebanon. They soon encountered a sizable convoy of Syrian supply and ammunition trucks and armored cars.

Thinking they were still in Israel, the Israelis fired on the first truck. It turned out to be a gasoline tanker. It exploded, causing a chain reaction. The second vehicle to explode was a truck full of hand grenades!

The Syrians ran in terror, abandoning their convoy. The 24 Israelis managed to drive all the Syrian vehicles back to Israel. When they reached the kibbutz, they found out where they had been. They also learned that the Arabs believed that Israel had invaded Lebanon! All the Arabs surrounding the kibbutz fled from Israel!

How could the lost Israeli soldiers have survived their trip? How did the first two Syrian vehicles happen to carry gasoline and hand grenades? Who orchestrated these things to save the kibbutz?

# 1967 THE SIX-DAY WAR

In 1967, Egypt, Syria, and Jordan ganged up against Israel. It started with Egypt's ships blockading the Strait of Tiran—an important passageway for Israel's shipping.

People all over the world held their breath for six days, but the war turned out to be a comedy of errors on the part of the Arabs. Bragging and miscommunication lost the war for them. Victory was mysteriously easy for Israel! So was their amazing bonus: They reclaimed some very sacred Jewish land. The question is: Was Israel so well equipped and talented that they won the war on their own, or did God intervene?

*Nasser's Big Mouth*

On June 5, Israel sent bombers on a preemptive strike, destroying the entire Egyptian air force as it lay helpless on the airfield! Egypt surrendered the next day. But instead of warning his allies, Syria and Jordan, Nasser was proclaiming victory over Israel on the radio!

His arrogant lie cost the Syrian army its air force as Israel proceeded to bomb them the next day.

It also affected Jordan. Israel had advised King Hussein that Israel would not strike Jordan unless Jordan struck first. Nasser lied to Hussein, bragging that Egypt was attacking Israel, so Jordan bombed West Jerusalem to back him up. As promised, Israel retaliated. Jordan surrendered the next day.

Israel claimed lots of territory from Egypt and Syria in one of the biggest military victories in history. In the south, Israel won the Sinai

Peninsula from Egypt; in the north, the Golan Heights from Syria; in the east, the West Bank of the Jordan River from Jordan. The West Bank was originally granted to Israel by the U.N. in 1948, but Jordan had annexed it as its own. (Translation: They stole it.)

The U.N. plan was that Jerusalem would be part of Israel, but as an international city. The city had been divided because half of it lay in the West Bank territory. The Old City, with its gates and walls, and the site of the Temple Mount had been out of Jewish possession for centuries. In 1948, Jordan grabbed the western half of Jerusalem, got away with it, and held the West Bank and western Jerusalem for 19 years.

In the Six-Day War, Israel just walked in and took back their most sacred city!

After just six days of fighting, Israeli forces broke through the enemy lines and were in a position to march on Cairo, Damascus, and Amman. A cease-fire was invoked on June 10.

Miraculously, in six days, the tiny Israeli army had completely routed the three Arab nations allied against them. Miraculously, Israel's casualties were very light: less than 800 soldiers were killed, compared to 13,000–15,000 Arab troops. These were the enemy forces against Israel:

Egypt: 270,000 soldiers, 1.400 tanks, 550 jets

Syria: 65,000 soldiers, 550 tanks, 120 jets

Jordan: 55,000 soldiers, 300 tanks, 40 jets

Lebanon: 12,000 soldiers, 130 tanks, 35 jets

Saudi Arabia: 50,000 soldiers, 100 tanks, 40 jets

Iraq: 75,000 soldiers, 630 tanks, 200 jets

Total enemy forces: 527,000 soldiers, 2,480 tanks, 985 jets

Total Jewish population in Israel in 1967: approximately 2 million

---

*Some trust in chariots and some in horses,*
*but we trust in the name of the LORD our God.*
PSALM 20:7

---

How did overwhelmingly outgunned Israel not only defend itself but end up with so much territory? How did the soldiers walk in and claim Jerusalem with no resistance?

*Testimony from the 1967 War*

Our friends William and Regina Kassler were on a cruise on the Norwegian Cruise Lines in 2005. They recorded their head waiter, Jacob Biton, as he relived his experience as an Israeli soldier in the Six-Day War:

*During the Six-Day War in 1967, on the fourth day of the war, two friends and I gained controlled over 300 Syrian troops, who surrendered as POWs. I remember telling my friends, "Look, we are outnumbered, and they can do anything to harm us." There were some other people with us, but there were only three of us visible [to the Syrians]. And we were controlling 300 people together.*

*Speaking in Arabic, I said to one of their officers, "Sir, why do you give up fighting?"*

*He said, "We see thousands of you. We are outnumbered. How are we going to beat you?"*

*Then I understood that the angels of the Lord were doing the fighting for us! I didn't ask any more questions. I got the message and swallowed my tongue! I said, "Yes, there are a lot of us here right now!"*

*It was a holy vision—they saw a lot of us!*

# 1973 YOM KIPPUR WAR

The easy victory of 1967 left Israel cocky and overconfident. They neglected their weapons and defense systems. Soldiers were undrilled and out of shape. Israel let down its guard.

Prime Minister Golda Meir saw the intelligence reports. Egypt and Syria were staging training exercises to prepare for war. Meir and Defense Minister Moshe Dayan didn't believe they would really be attacked! They chose to rely on Israel's elite air force. Meir and Dayan disregarded secret warnings from Jordan's King Hussein and from the

CIA. Even Egypt's President Anwar Sadat issued repeated warnings and requests for negotiations. Meir and Dayan ignored them all.

In October 6, 1973, Egypt and Syria launched a surprise attack against Israel on the holiest day of the Jewish calendar: Yom Kippur, the Day of Atonement. Knowing that Israel could not mobilize for defense with everything closed, including television and radio, they attacked on two fronts. Egypt crossed the Suez Canal to reclaim the Sinai Peninsula, while Syria attacked the Golan Heights.

As usual, God must have intervened for Israel to prevail or even to survive. So many factors were against Israel. They faced a vastly uneven ratio of arms and troops. While Syria had five divisions with over 45,000 troops, 1,500 tanks, and 1,000 artillery pieces, Israel only had 6,000 troops, 170 tanks, and 60 artillery pieces.

Egypt put out 500–700 tanks to Israel's 180! In the first minute of attack, 10,500 pieces of Arab artillery were fired.

Israel's air force was outnumbered 2–1.

In the Golan Heights, Egypt had 25,000 soldiers. Israel had 500!

The Bar Lev Line was a warning and defense perimeter along the border between Israel and Sinai. It was made up of 31 small forts, each with gas flamethrowers to respond to any Egyptian attack. The border defenses were down because of the poor emergency preparedness. When the attack actually came:

- The gas flamethrowers were out of gas!
- Troops had not been drilled; equipment had not been checked and was not working. A recent drill testing the Bar Lev Line's response to attack had been a total failure. Nothing was done to improve readiness.
- The forts were in the process of being replaced by mobile defense forces. Half of the forts were closed and half had just a few sentries. Only 500 troops were stationed along the entire Bar Lev Line.
- Dumb intelligence: Bugs had been planted beneath Cairo streets to warn of attack plans. The bugs were never activated.

- Massive traffic jams of Israelis fleeing from the coming invasion prevented troops from reaching the border.
- No tanks or armored vehicles were at the Line. The sentries faced the enemy, stranded and helpless. Many were killed, as were many who were sent to rescue them.

Russia supplied massive arms, planes, and supplies to Egypt and Syria. The U.S. promised to match that, but did not send Israel anything until November, a month after the war!

Israel's top military leaders refused to authorize decisive action that would have led to victory and entered into conflicts and contradictions. General Ariel Sharon wanted to cross the Suez Canal into Egypt for a counterattack. He was ordered not to do it.

Sharon finally got permission to cross the canal and surround the Egyptian army. The bridges that were needed to cross the canal never arrived. Sharon was ordered to stay put, but he disobeyed his orders and pressed forward with the attack. Thanks to Sharon, but not thanks to his superiors, Egypt was finally defeated.

Egypt staged a second offensive but advanced too far, ahead of the cover of their SAM missiles. Israel was able to wipe them out! After Israeli forces crossed the canal, Egypt's Chief of Staff Shazly wanted to move his troops around to box in the Israelis. Anwar Sadat refused, thinking that it would look like a withdrawal or a sign of weakness. That foolishness allowed the Israelis to destroy a whole brigade of Egyptian tanks. When Shazly insisted on his plan, Sadat fired him. Shazly's plan would have worked, but Sadat's pride cost Egypt the war.

Israel won the war in spite of many blunders. Egypt's two blunders caused its defeat! God once again helped Israel. This war was not won by human cleverness! Again in the Yom Kippur War there was a miracle against all odds.

A folk hero arose from the Yom Kippur War. One man held off Syrian tanks all night to become known throughout Israel as the Zvika Force. Here is an account from the *Jerusalem Post*:

*Lieutenant Zvika Greengold was from an Israeli kibbutz.*

*He was traveling alone, hitchhiking back from a course
he had taken for company commanders. Reporting for
duty at the front at Nafekh, he was told that there were no
tanks available, so he helped with the wounded. Soon two
Centurion tanks arrived at the camp. He had to clear
out two dead crewmen from one of them, then he took off
down the Tapline Road toward the action.*

*For the next twenty hours, Zvika Force, as he came to be
known on the radio net, fought running battles with Syrian
tanks—sometimes alone, sometimes as part of a larger unit,
changing tanks half a dozen times as they were knocked
out. He was wounded and burned but stayed in action
and repeatedly showed up at critical moments from an
unexpected direction to change the course of a skirmish. At
one point, in one of the tanks he took over, the driver bolted
because his nerves could no longer take the succession of hair-
raising encounters.*[33]

Another story also highlights the miracles that occurred during the
Yom Kippur War:

*Effie Eitam was commander of a group of Isreali commandos
on the Golan Heights. He was given orders to go miles behind
enemy lines and take the Syrian division headquarters. When
he finally arrived at this location, a very dangerous mission
no doubt, his commandos went into the bunkers and started
killing generals and their guards. There was smoke in the
corridors everywhere from explosions of hand grenades.*

*All of a sudden from the smoke appeared a white dove that
flew onto Effie's shoulder. Try as he might, he could not get it
to leave. Every time he pushed it off, she would fly right back
to his shoulder. She stayed on his shoulder through 10 days of
the most intense fighting of the Yom Kippur War. Both he and
his unit had supernatural protection and not one soldier was*

> *injured. When Eitam's unit was sent back to Israel for a rest,*
> *the dove left and he never saw her again.*[34]

The U.N. ordered a cease-fire at Egypt's request, but as Israel's soldiers headed home, the Egyptians fired on them. Israel therefore ignored the cease-fire and tried to take Suez City. An international outcry arose over Israel's violations of the cease-fire. As usual, no one objected that it was Egypt who started it by shooting at Israeli forces!

Russia believed that the Israelis would capture Cairo, while the U.S. thought that Russia was sending nuclear weapons to Egypt. The showdown finally ended with a genuine cease-fire.

The incompetence of Israel's government and military leaders should have caused Israel to be defeated. The people's loss of confidence in their leaders led to the downfall of Golda Meir and her administration.

God was sovereign in the 1973 war. He brought Israel the victory in spite of human foolishness.

## 1991 GULF WAR

The Persian Gulf War took place between January 17–February 28, 1991, and was the response to Iraq's invasion of Kuwait to acquire its rich oil fields. When Saddam Hussein ignored the U.S. ultimatum to withdraw from Kuwait, the U.S. and other allies attacked Iraq with computer precision air strikes.

Hussein used the war as an excuse to attack Israel with his Scud missiles. U.S. Patriot missiles shot down many Scuds over Israel. There was damage from the Scuds, but it seemed as though angels were steering them. Either the Iraqis were really lousy shots, or God intervened. The lack of damage made no logical sense. Most of the rockets fell harmlessly to the ground as miracles abounded.

The list of miracles is long! Israel was an innocent bystander in the Gulf War. God moved mightily to protect His chosen people who were in harm's way.

One woman summed it up: "If you live in Israel and don't believe in miracles, you're just not being realistic."[35]

During the Gulf War, Iraq launched 39 Scud missiles toward Israel, dropping over 10 tons of explosives. Fifteen thousand Israeli properties were damaged: 10,992 apartments, 235 houses, and 3,773 other buildings.

Only 13 people died. Two were killed directly by missiles. Eleven died from heart attacks or from incorrect use of their gas masks. Considering the number of Scuds fired, only 13 dead can only be called a miracle! It can't be called luck!

In contrast, just one Scud missile dropped onto a U.S. army barrack in Saudi Arabia killed 28 U.S. soldiers on February 25, 1991.

There are dozens and dozens of stories that detail how God saved His people from the Scuds. The following are a sample:

- My cousin lived in Haifa during the war. She wrote to me about an old man who was sitting at his kitchen table reading his Bible. He left it open when he left for evening prayers at the synagogue. A missile fell on his house, landing dead center on the open pages of his Bible.
- A man and his wife, Shalom and Jaquelyn H., although non-observant, respected Torah scholars, had recently replaced their *mezuzah* scrolls. A *mezuzah* is the small decorative tube that goes on the doorpost of a Jewish home. Inside is a tiny rolled-up paper with Bible verses. Their apartment building was destroyed by a Scud. Their apartment was in shreds. Even the doorposts came off their frames. The only things left undamaged were the mezuzahs on the doors. The couple was unharmed![36]
- A civil defense official described what he saw: "In a second a portion of Lai Street was turned into desolation. I was in a number of places that were hit by missiles, and each time I can't understand how people came out alive from such destruction. Someone up there is watching over them, otherwise there is no explanation as to what took place here tonight."
- An elderly woman was woken up and led from her apartment by her neighbor just moments before it was hit by a missile.[37]

- A baker ran out of flour on the night before *Shabbat*, so he left his bakery to buy some. Moments later a missile flattened the bakery.[38]
- One missile landed in the middle of a street. The houses on either side were completely demolished. Rescuers pulled an elderly resident from one of the houses. He was not hurt at all. No one was home across the street.[39]
- Rescue teams heard a man calling for help from the rubble of his house. He was pulled out without a scratch. When the missile fell, he had been standing between his two dogs. They were both killed.[40]
- At 2 a.m., sirens rang out. An elderly lady was invited next door by her neighbors, so she wouldn't be alone. As they passed between the two front doors, a missile fell in the alley between them and destroyed both houses while they were all outside. The frame of the entranceway protected them.[41]

Saddam ranted and raved that he would use nonconventional weapons on Israel. Fearing a chemical or biological attack, Israeli civil defense instructed the people to set up small rooms completely sealed off with plastic and tape. Every person in Israel was issued a gas mask. When they heard the air raid siren, everyone was to rush into their sealed rooms and put on their gas masks.

The seasonal rains in Israel are usually in November. It never rained in November that year. Suddenly on January 17, 1991, the first day of the war, rain came down in torrents. Rain continued almost without ceasing for the next four to six weeks, along with high winds. According to U.S. military sources, the Iraqis decided that using chemical weapons would not be smart, because the strong winds were blowing from Israel directly toward Iraq! The same phenomenon was observed in Kuwait (900 kilometers to the east), where wind patterns had shifted from their normal direction for that season and were also blowing toward Iraq according to an article in the February *Jerusalem Post*.

God used the sealed rooms, or lack of them, to save many of His people. He gave Israel instructions through the prophet Isaiah:

*Go, my people, enter your rooms and shut the doors*
*behind you; hide yourselves for a little while*
*until his wrath has passed by.*

Isaiah 26:20

Here are numerous stories of miracles related to sealed rooms and bomb shelters:

- A bomb shelter was demolished by a missile. Because people were in their sealed rooms, the shelter was empty. If they had not been expecting chemical weapons, there would have been about 50 people in the shelter.[42]
- Many apartments were badly damaged or destroyed, but the sealed rooms were untouched.[43]
- A man named Nissim escaped from his sealed room as the rest of his apartment burned.[44]
- A man was leaning against a closet door in his sealed room. A missile exploded, knocking him into the closet. The apartment and the sealed room were smashed, but he was safe and sound in the closet![45]
- A family was in their sealed room with their 18-month-old baby. The explosion knocked the wall down on the baby, who was protected by the plastic infant tent that the government gave babies instead of gas masks. The baby was not hurt at all.[46]
- One family didn't trust their sealed room and chose to race to the bomb shelter in case of attack. When they heard the siren, they could not find the key needed to enter the shelter, so they ran back to their sealed room. A missile destroyed the shelter, but they were safe and sound.[47]
- Two families ran for the bomb shelter. They couldn't find the key to the first one, so they ran to another one nearby. The first one was destroyed.[48]

Then there are dozens of stories of missiles that inexplicably failed to detonate or that did relatively little damage. For instance, two missiles at an Israeli army base went down the airshaft of a building with about 30 apartments. In another case, a missile that landed on a major Tel Aviv street thoroughfare on *Shabbat* morning failed to detonate. Several missiles aimed at Israel fell into the sea to the west or were blown off course by a strong wind. Two missiles aimed at the IDF base in the Negev desert landed without causing damage.

A national day of prayer took place on February 27. The main meeting, held at Jerusalem's Great Synagogue, was attended by Prime Minister Yitzhak Shamir, President Haim Herzog, Religious Affairs Minister Avner Shaki, and both chief rabbis. On February 28, the eve of Purim, Iraq agreed to a U.N. cease-fire plan.

The last all clear siren was followed by the announcement that the war was over. It came over the air in Hebrew, English, Ethiopian, French, Russian, and Romanian, proving that Jewish people had come home to Israel from all over the world.[49] CNN showed people removing the plastic and tape from their sealed rooms as children danced around in *Purim* costumes.

Was it a coincidence that the Gulf War ended on the holiday of Purim? Purim is the celebration of the survival of the Jewish people as told in the book of Esther. The Jews had been taken captive by Babylon. Persia then conquered Babylon, so the Jews came under the rule of King Xerxes (also called Ahasuerus). The wicked official Haman convinced the king to kill all the Jews in the kingdom. Queen Esther, who was secretly Jewish, begged the king for the lives of her people. Instead of the Jews dying, Haman was hanged. As I used to sing in our *Purim* play, "The evil that you plotted, well, it came back to you!"

In 1991, the people of Israel were once again delivered from evil; this time from Saddam Hussein.

## INTIFADA: 2000 ON

Early in the Intifada terrorist attacks against Israel that began in 2000, the Palestinian towns of Jenin and Shechem saw fierce battles. In the town of Jenin was a miracle just as dramatic as those in the Old Testament.

The Palestinians had the whole town booby-trapped with explosives. Their men, women, and children were wired up as suicide bombers. They waited in ambush in the narrow alleyways for the Israeli soldiers, who were ordered to take the town by foot, house by house. One morning 13 Israeli soldiers died in a sudden explosion. Things seemed hopeless.

Remember how God caused the sun to stand still for Joshua? God used the natural forces to save Israel. Could that kind of miracle happen again?

In desperation, an Israeli commander shouted over the bullhorn to the Palestinians that unless they surrendered immediately, Israel was sending a squadron of F-16 bombers to destroy them all! The Israelis never dreamed that the enemy would believe their bluff. It was just their last shot. Surely no one would believe that Israel would attack and kill innocent civilians!

But God intervened. An ear-splitting explosion went off overhead. Palestinians and Israelis all dropped to the ground. They awaited the shock waves to follow the explosion, but there were none, because what they had just heard and seen was lightning and thunder! As everyone stood back up, they saw a second huge lightning bolt, simultaneous with thunder.

Everyone knows that when a thunderstorm is approaching, the lightning and thunder are not synchronized. We see the lightning first. As kids, we learned to judge how far away the storm was by counting the seconds between the lightning and the thunder. But that night in Jenin, the sudden lightning and thunder shook the town like a massive bomb.

The Palestinians crawled out from their hiding places with white flags, laying down their weapons and their bodies on the ground! When the Israelis asked them why they gave up so easily, they exclaimed, "It was those F-16s dropping their bombs," one of them answered. "You can't fight against a plane."

## THE 2006 LEBANON WAR

The conflict, also known as the Second Lebanon War, started on July 12, 2006, when Hezbollah militants fired rockets at Israeli border towns, and continued until a U.N.-brokered cease-fire went into effect in the morning on August 14, 2006, though it formally ended on September 8, 2006, when Israel lifted its naval blockade of Lebanon.

Hezbollah terrorists attacked northern Israel with more than 120 rockets throughout northern Israel, but only four people suffered injuries. One person was wounded seriously, three others suffered light wounds, and several others were treated for shock.

A Hezbollah-fired rocket exploded less than 100 yards away from the municipal offices of the city of Acre (Akko), north of Haifa, while the mayor was holding an emergency meeting. Mayor Shimon Lankri said those at the meeting were able to watch the *Katyusha* (missile) as it exploded. No one was injured in the blast.

One of the rockets in the massive attack on Haifa around noon exploded several meters from a road bridge. The impact of the explosion shattered all the windows of a nearby Egged public bus, which was empty of passengers, because the driver had reached the end of the line when the Katyusha hit. He suffered moderate wounds.

Before the Second Lebanon War, but during a Gaza reengagement, one of the three *Kassams* (rockets) fired at Sderot on a Sunday morning scored a direct hit on a classroom in the Netiv Yeshivati branch of the local religious high school just as the students were coming up to the classroom. "The students were on their way to the classroom after finishing morning prayers," one person said, "and the classroom was still locked. Some students were waiting outside, and the teacher was on his way up—and that's when all of a sudden the rocket crashed in, hitting the teacher's chair. The teacher was very emotional, seeing that it had crashed exactly where he would have been sitting minutes later." One person was treated for shock.[50]

One of the two Katyushas that hit the northern city of Safed on Sunday afternoon landed in the only house still under construction in the Kiryat Breslav neighborhood. The other hit an empty area on the hillside above the houses.[51]

On May 8, 2006, Kiryat Yam was hit by Hezbollah rockets and suffered casualties and property damage. A Katyusha fell only three feet from an *ulpan* classroom at the Sapir Absorption Center in Kiryat Yam, where, just one hour before, 100 Ethiopian immigrant children were taking a break from the stifling bomb shelter.[52]

On July 20, 2006, a Katyusha slammed on the grounds of a Chabad-Lubavitch synagogue in the northern city of Nahariya, blowing out all the building's windows and doors. All in all, no one was hurt, not even the Torah scrolls. "It's a miracle," reported Rabbi Yisroel Butman. "We managed to save the Torahs. It's a terrible mess. The loss of even one Jewish life is too many, but considering the number of rockets Hezbollah has launched at Nahariya, it is amazing there have not been more losses. Do you know how many miraculous stories I could tell, just from the past week?"[53]

An investigation made by the DEBKA organization from August 22, 2006, wondered why Israeli Prime Minister Olmert held off the ground campaign until it was too late. They suggested that it was because he promised Condoleezza Rice, who pulled the strings in the background to stick to an air offensive.[54]

An open letter of grievances signed by officers and men of the Israeli army's crack Alexandroni Brigade shocked and still puzzles the entire nation. The lack of clear decisions was manifested, they said, in the failure to act, the nonimplementation of operational plans, and the cancellation amid combat of missions assigned the unit. The result was that the unit was deployed too long in hostile country without any operational purpose for reasons that were unprofessional and, moreover, held back from making contact with the enemy. In every stage of the war, cold feet were evident in decision-making. That was one of the riddles of the Lebanon War.

The DEBKA file investigation has uncovered some facts that would help explain some of the mishaps. The knife-edge threat that caught the Israeli army unprepared was welcomed in Washington. Our sources close to the Bush administration have learned that Secretary of State Condoleezza Rice embraced the opening for an Israeli offensive against Hezbollah in Lebanon. Vice President Dick Cheney also favored an Israeli air strike, but worried about the lack of an Israeli plan for a parallel ground offensive. One of his aides later expressed the view that Olmert and Halutz had been cautioned that air offensives unaccompanied by ground assaults never achieved strategic goals, as the Americans discovered after bombing Baghdad at the start of the Iraq war in 2003.

But the Israeli prime minister and chief of staff insisted that the air force was able to inflict a shock defeat on Hezbollah and produce a fast and cheap victory.

U.S. Secretary of Defense Donald Rumsfeld was leery about any Israeli military offensive against Hezbollah, fearing complications for the U.S. army in Iraq at the peak of a surging sectarian civil war. But Olmert talked Rice into asking President George W. Bush to back the air offensive. The president acceded, only laying down two basic conditions: Israel must confine itself to an air campaign; before embarking on a ground offensive, a further American go-ahead would be required. The second was a promise to spare Lebanon's civilian infrastructure and only go for Hezbollah's positions and installations.

These conditions were accepted by the prime minister. The first explains why Israel's ground forces were held ready in bases for three long weeks rather than being sent into battle until the last stage. By then, the air force offensive had proved a long way short of fast and cheap; worse, it had been ineffectual.

The second condition accounts for another of the war's enigmas: Israeli forces were not allowed to destroy buildings known to be occupied by Hezbollah teams firing anti-tank rockets, because it would have meant destroying Lebanese infrastructure. This brought Israeli forces into extreme danger; they were forced to come back again and again to repeat cleansing operations in villages and towns close to the Israeli border, such as Maroun a-Ras, Bint Jubeil, and Atia a-Chaab. This exposed them to Hezbollah's attrition tactics at the cost of painful casualties.

Only in the third week of the war, when the Bush administration saw the Israeli air force had failed to bring Hezbollah to collapse, and the campaign would have to be salvaged in a hurry, did Rice give the green light for ground troops to go in en masse to try and finish off the Shiite terrorist group. Then, too, an American stipulation was imposed: Israel troops must not reach the Litani River.

The Israel army did embark on a tardy wide-scale push to the Litani River and as far as Nabatia and Arnoun, but was soon cut short in its tracks. American spy satellites spotted the advance, and Olmert was cautioned by Washington to hold his horses. This last disastrous order released the welter of conflicting, incomprehensible orders that stirred up the entire chain of command from the heads of the IDF's Northern command down to the officers in the field. Operational orders designed to meet tactical combat situations were scrapped in mid execution and new directives tumbled down the chute from above. Soldiers later complained that in one day, they were jerked into unreasoned actions by four to six contrary instructions.

According to our sources, Olmert kept his exchanges with Condoleezza Rice close to his chest and members of his cabinet and high army command firmly out of the process. The prime minister even kept the chief of staff out of the picture and did not explain why he was called on to chop and change tactics in the heat of war. Olmert's absolute compliance with Rice's directives without fully comprehending their military import threw Israel's entire war campaign into disorder.

# 10

# *The Peace* Process

I srael gave back the Sinai to Egypt in 1957; 10 years later, Egypt used that very place to launch war against Israel! The same goes for the Golan Heights and the Gaza. Hasn't history already and repeatedly proven that land giveaways don't work?

Why does Israel never wait for actual peace before it grants concessions? Only defeating an enemy brings peace! Appeasement makes Israel seem weak and easy to defeat. As war after war has shown, without military victory there is no peace.

Israeli and American leaders know the Muslims' goal: to annihilate Israel and take over the area. Why do they act as though the Arabs might keep their promises? Even the U.N. recognized that giving land away to bring peace did not work. U.N. Security Council Resolution 242 called for Israel's concession of land only after a formal peace was secured. That resolution seems to have been forgotten, even by the U.N.

The most futile talks were with the late Yasser Arafat, founder of the PLO and the originator of terrorism in the twentieth century. Arafat actually won the Nobel Peace Prize for participating! After shaking hands on peace agreements between the PLO and Israel, Yasser Arafat would turn to his people to remind them of what Mohammad, the founder of Islam, taught: to make peace with their enemies until they can build up their army and weapons to beat them. Then you attack your enemy by surprise and get the victory.

I personally do not see a true truce being set here. What I believe will take place is Osama bin Laden will exercise what is called the *Quraysh* Model of Meccan conquest: "Three years after the battle of Badr, a 10,000-man Meccan army again laid siege to Medina. The *Quraysh* tribe of Mecca was not able to conquer Medina, and Mohammad was not strong enough to defeat them; so Mohammad signed a 10-year treaty of nonaggression with Mecca. Less than a year later, Mohammad had built up his army. He stormed Mecca by surprise and conquered it, thus making himself ruler of the city of his birth."[55]

## APPEASEMENT

Why does the peace process continue when the Arabs don't hold up their end of the bargain? Every agreement ends up the same way: Israel will give up land, and the Arabs will cease all violence. Why does Israel always go first? They give away land, but the Arabs don't stop the violence. How can any peace talks be taken seriously? Despite reality, we still hear about the hopes for peace.

Those highly hyped peace hopes are orchestrated by Israel's friend, the U.S., and by the three other members of the quartet. Since 2003, they have been behind the Road Map peace talks: the U.S., the E.U., the U.N., and Russia.

The leaders of the Israeli government believe they can broker peace with their enemies. Hopes for peace are based on the premise that Israel can appease the Arab nations, who will theoretically stop their terrorism and aggression, even though they are bound by their religion to kill every single Jew and eliminate the nation of Israel.

Appeasing the enemy has never worked. When an aggressive nation tries to conquer the world, appeasement plays into their hands. Why would it stop them? Appeasement achieves their goals for them, helping them take over Israel piece by piece! (Can they trade a piece for peace?)

Appeasement really says to your enemy, "I am afraid of you! I don't think I can defeat you, so if I'm very, very nice to you, maybe you'll go away!" Back in the schoolyard, the only way to stop a bully was to stand up tall and refuse to be intimidated.

World War II would have been very short if England and the Allies had fought back earlier instead of trying to appease Germany. Hitler was not stopped by politeness! Millions of Jews might not have died! Then, as now, a forceful aggressor can only be stopped by force.

Are Israel's Arab neighbors to be compared to Hitler? Followers of Islam believe they are required by Allah to take over the world and force everyone to become a Muslim. Their holy book, the Koran, commands them to kill all the "people of the Book"—Jews and Christians.

When we try to appease the Muslims, they laugh at us! They have no intention of abiding by any peace agreement. After all, what do they call the campaign of violence? Jihad, a holy war!

## BORDERS

Does Israel rightfully own the territories it won from the Arabs, or should she give them back? Is she "occupying" the West Bank and Jerusalem? Israel never initiated a war or tried to conquer any other country. She simply and miraculously defended herself. As a result, she won territory from her enemies in every war. What other country would be expected to return land it won in a war, especially when they were the defenders, not the aggressors! Israel won the land in self-defense.

Not only was the land won by Israel, it was granted to her by God in the Bible.

## THE CONTESTED AREAS

Ownership of the following areas are contested by the Arabs:

## Golan Heights

The Golan Heights is in the northeastern edge of Israel, bordering Lebanon and Syria. On its western edge is a high plateau along the Jordan River, overlooking Israeli settlements. Israel captured the Golan Heights from Syria in the 1967 Six-Day War. Syria took it back for a short time during the 1973 Yom Kippur War, but Israel won it back again. Throughout the time that Syria controlled the Golan Heights, they used the high vantage points to bombard civilians in nearby Israel. That is why control of this area is vital for Israel's self-defense.

## West Bank

The West Bank is more commonly known as Judea and Samaria. It is a massive slice of central Israel that borders the Jordan River and makes up about a quarter of the land mass of Israel! It is filled with towns we recognize from the Bible: Bethlehem, Hebron, Jericho, Shechem, and Shiloh. The western border of the West Bank cuts through Jerusalem. The part of the city that lies in the West Bank is called East Jerusalem, which means it is like having hostile enemies right across the street!

Before 1948, the West Bank was part of Israel/Palestine—part of the British mandate and not a separate area. In 1948, Jordan captured the West Bank, where the population is predominantly Palestinian with some Jewish settlements, and held it until the 1967 Six-Day War, where Moshe Dayan stopped commandos from blowing up the Dome of the Rock in Jerusalem, saying, "We've done enough!"

The western border of the West Bank is also very close to Tel Aviv. Jerusalem and Tel Aviv would be practically indefensible if the Arabs ruled the West Bank.

---

*"But I will not take the whole kingdom out of*
*Solomon's hand; I have made him ruler all the days of*
*his life for the sake of David my servant, whom I chose and*
*who observed my commands and statutes. I will take the*
*kingdom from his son's hands and give you ten tribes. I will*
*give one tribe to his son so that David my servant may always*

*have a lamp before me in Jerusalem,*
*the city where I chose to put my Name."*
1 KINGS 11:34–36

*Rehoboam son of Solomon was king in Judah.*
*He was forty-one years old when he became king,*
*and he reigned seventeen years in Jerusalem,*
*the city the LORD had chosen out of all the tribes of*
*Israel in which to put his Name.*
1 KINGS 14:21

*Many peoples will come and say, "Come, let us go up to the*
*mountain of the LORD, to the house of the God of Jacob. He will*
*teach us his ways, so that we may walk in his paths." The law will*
*go out from Zion, the word of the LORD from Jerusalem.*
ISAIAH 2:3

*The moon will be abashed, the sun ashamed; for the LORD*
*Almighty will reign on Mount Zion and in Jerusalem,*
*and before its elders, gloriously.*
ISAIAH 24:23

---

Yeshua wept as He looked out at Jerusalem, saying, "O Jerusalem, Jerusalem, you who kill the prophets and stone those sent to you, how often I have longed to gather your children together, as a hen gathers her chicks under her wings, but you were not willing" (Matthew 23:37).

It sounds like God wants Israel to keep Jerusalem at all costs! It must always be their capital city, because it is the place that God has chosen. It is not just a city, a patriotic symbol, or a rallying point. It is the supernatural home of the Jewish people.

### Sinai Peninsula

A formerly contested area, the Sinai Peninsula differs from the others in that it was originally part of Egypt. After Egypt's blockade of the

Suez Canal in 1956, Israel took over the Sinai to stop the blockade. Afterward, the area was protected by U.N. troops.

The 1967 Six-Day War began with Egypt blockading the canal and evicting the U.N. troops. Again, Israel routed them and retook the Sinai. The 1979 Camp David Accords saw Israel return the Sinai Peninsula to Egypt.

In this rare instance, peace continued between Israel and Egypt. Sadly, it cost the life of Egyptian President Anwar Sadat. Militant Muslim Arabs assassinated him for daring to make peace with Israel.

*Gaza Strip*

The Gaza Strip is a very small area in the southwest, bordering Egypt. Israel captured Gaza in the 1967 Six-Day War. The 1993 Oslo Accords resulted in part of the Gaza Strip going to the Palestinians. In August 2005, Israel disengaged by forcibly removing all Jewish residents from the Gaza.

## HISTORY OF THE PEACE PROCESS

The meetings between the Israelis, the Arab states, and the nations trying to help have been going on for decades. The only lasting result was with Egypt.

Until World War I, the Middle East was ruled by the Turkish Ottoman Empire. The Arab tribes were nomads in the desert wilderness. Something happened in the early 1900s that forged them into nations—Oil! Rich oil reserves brought England sniffing around. The huge British oil companies wanted control of all those oil-rich desert lands.

When World War I erupted, it presented an opportunity! England, in cahoots with France, decided to rally the many Arab tribes into one huge army that could overthrow the Ottoman Turks and gain control. If England and France helped them, the Arabs would remain faithful to them afterward. The job was done from 1916–1918, under the command of Lt. Col. Thomas Edward.

This was a secret understanding between the governments of Britain and France, spelling out who controlled what in the Middle East after World War I. The border between Syria and Iraq is still the result of this agreement. French diplomat François Georges-Picot and British Mark Sykes were the negotiators.

Britain took control of what would become Jordan and Iraq and a small area around Haifa. France controlled southeastern Turkey, northern Iraq, Syria, and Lebanon.

Palestine was a temporary derogatory name given to Israel, while Britain, France, and Russia decided how to divide it up.

## The Balfour Declaration

On November 2, 1917, British Foreign Secretary Arthur James Balfour sent a letter to Lord Walter Rothschild, a leader of the British Jewish community, for the Zionist Federation about this issue: Should there be a Jewish state in "Palestine"?

In this letter, the British government declared its support for the establishment in Palestine of "a national home for the Jewish people." This letter became known as the Balfour Declaration.[56]

The letter reported the vote in the British Cabinet to allow a Jewish "national home" in Palestine, providing the existing non-Jewish communities maintained their rights.

The agreement was later expanded to include Italy and Russia. Russia was to receive Armenia and parts of Kurdistan, while the Italians would get certain Aegean islands and a sphere of influence around Izmir in southwest Anatolia. The Italian presence in Anatolia as well as the division of the Arab lands was later formalized in the Treaty of Sèvres in 1920.

The Russian Revolution of 1917 led to Russia being denied its claims in the Ottoman Empire. At the same time, Lenin released a copy of the confidential Sykes-Picot Agreement as well as other treaties, causing great embarrassment among the allies and growing distrust among the Arabs.

Why wouldn't the Arabs mistrust these countries? They were plotting to set up puppet Arab governments that they could control, for the sake of oil.

## Paris Peace Treaty

At the end of World War I, a meeting took place to determine the future of Middle East. It resulted in the Faisal-Weizmann Agreement that was signed on January 3, 1919, by Emir Feisal (son of the King of Hejaz and who become king of Syria) and Chaim Weizmann (later president of the World Zionist Organization). Weizmann signed the agreement on behalf of the Zionist Organization, while Faisal signed on behalf of the short-lived Arab kingdom of Hedjaz.

It was taken as part of the 1919 Paris Peace Conference, settling disputes stemming from World War I. It was a short-lived agreement for Arab-Jewish cooperation on the development of a Jewish homeland in Palestine and an Arab nation in a large part of the Middle East. It was an accord that climaxed years of negotiations and ceaseless shuttles between the Middle East and the capitals of Western Europe and that promised to usher in an era of peace and cooperation between the two principal ethnic groups of Palestine: Arabs and Jews.

As result of this agreement, both parties, Israel and Palestine, were to conduct all relations by cordial goodwill and understanding, to work together to encourage immigration of Jews into Palestine on a large scale, while protecting the rights of the Arab peasants and tenant farmers, and to safeguard the free practice of religious observances. The Muslim holy places were to be under Muslim control.

The Zionist movement undertook to assist the Arab residents of Palestine and the future Arab state to develop their natural resources and establish a growing economy.

The boundaries between an Arab State and Palestine were to be determined by a commission after the Paris Peace Conference. The parties committed to carrying into effect the Balfour Declaration, calling for a Jewish national home in Palestine. Disputes were to be submitted to the British government for arbitration.

They discussed how Arabs and Jews would work together toward establishing a homeland for the Jews in Palestine.[57] We all know how that went!

## The Palestine Mandate

On June 24, 1922, the League of Nations agreed on how much power Britain would have as the mandatory, or administrator, over Palestine. The area was called the British Mandate of Palestine. The mandate was to be terminated in 1948, and it was when the nation of Israel was born.

Note: All residents of the Palestine Mandate were called Palestinians. They were Jews, Christians, Arabs, and others. Only when the PLO started its propaganda campaign did Palestinian refer only to Arab former residents of Israel.

## Summits, Resolutions, Letters, and Proposals

In 1949, negotiations were conducted under the aegis of U.N. Mediator Ralph Bunche to end hostilities between Israel and its four neighboring enemies. These armistice agreements took some land that had been given to Palestine, or Israel, and handed it to Jordan and Syria. The Gaza Strip stayed with Egypt. By June 1949, armistice was reached between Israel and each of its enemies.

On September 13, 1964, the second Arab summit conference was held in Alexandria. There they declared the goal of eliminating Israel and made concrete decisions regarding unification of army commands, increased size of armed forces, and diversion of the waters of the Jordan before they reached the Sea of Galilee, in Syria and Lebanon.

In 1967, U.N. Security Council Resolution 242 was adopted following the Six-Day War, calling for a negotiated peace and Israeli withdrawal from territories conquered in the Six-Day War.

In 1967, the Khartoum Resolutions followed the Six-Day War. It came from an Arab summit meeting in Khartoum that rejected the possibility of peace or negotiations with Israel.

In 1968, U.N. Security Council Resolution 252 was called on Israel to halt its plans for unification of Jerusalem.

In 1989, after the Palestine National Council (the PLO), Israel accepted two U.N. Resolutions. Under U.S. pressure, Israel issued a peace plan for negotiations with the Palestinians, but not with the PLO.

In 1993, Yitzhak Rabin and Yasser Arafat exchanged letters prior to the signing of the Oslo Declaration of Principles. Arafat promised to stop PLO violence and to amend their charter that called for "driving Israel into the sea." Rabin promised to work toward peace and for providing a normal life for Palestinians.

## The Camp David Accords

Twelve days of secret negotiations at Camp David that began on September 17, 1978, resulted in the Camp David Accords that were signed by Egyptian President Anwar El Sadat and Israeli Prime Minister Menachem Begin at the White House and witnessed by U.S. President Jimmy Carter. These agreements led to the 1979 Israel-Egypt Peace Treaty.

There were two agreements: a Framework for Peace in the Middle East and a Framework for the Conclusion of a Peace Treaty between Egypt and Israel. The agreements and the peace treaty were both accompanied by "side-letters" of understanding between Egypt and the U.S. and Israel and the U.S.

The first agreement had three parts. The first part was a framework for negotiations to establish an autonomous self-governing authority in the West Bank and the Gaza Strip and to fully implement U.N. Security Council Resolution 242. It was less clear than the agreements concerning the Sinai and was later interpreted differently by Israel, Egypt, and the U.S. The fate of Jerusalem was deliberately excluded from this agreement.

The second part dealt with Egyptian-Israeli relations, the real content being in the second agreement. The third part, "Associated Principles," declared principles that should apply to relations between Israel and all of its Arab neighbors.

The second agreement outlined a basis for the peace treaty six months later, in particular deciding the future of the Sinai Peninsula. Israel agreed to withdraw its armed forces from the Sinai, evacuate its 4,500 civilian inhabitants, and restore it to Egypt in return for normal diplomatic relations with Egypt, guarantees of freedom of passage through the Suez

Canal and other nearby waterways (such as the Straits of Tiran), and a restriction on the forces Egypt could place on the Sinai Peninsula.

Israel also agreed to limit its forces a smaller distance from the Egyptian border and to guarantee free passage between Egypt and Jordan. With the withdrawal, Israel also returned Egypt's Abu Rudeis oil fields in western Sinai, which contained long term, commercially productive wells.

The agreement also resulted in the U.S. committing to several billion dollars worth of annual subsidies to the governments of both Israel and Egypt, subsidies which continue to this day, and are given as a mixture of grants and aid packages committed to purchasing U.S. materials.[58]

Israel withdrew from the Sinai Peninsula. The West Bank and Gaza Strip were put under military supervision. Israel remained at peace with Egypt. A framework agreement was signed, calling for peace in the Middle East and peace between Egypt and Israel.

The Middle East Framework was not implemented, but some of its principles were incorporated into later negotiations with the Palestinians and Syrians.

*Israel-Egypt Peace Treaty*

The 1979 Egypt-Israel Peace Treaty was signed after intense negotiation in Washington, D.C., on March 26, 1979—16 months after Egyptian President Anwar Sadat's visit to Israel in 1977. It was based on the Camp David Accords, after extensive shuttle diplomacy by President Jimmy Carter.

The main features of the treaty were the mutual recognition of each country by the other—actually Egypt was the first Arab country to officially recognize Israel. It caused the cessation of the state of war that had existed since the 1948 Arab-Israeli War, and the complete withdrawal by Israel of its armed forces and civilians from the rest of the Sinai Peninsula, which Israel had captured during the Six-Day War.

The agreement also provided for the free passage of Israeli ships through the Suez Canal and recognition of the Strait of Tiran, the Gulf of Aqaba, and the Taba-Rafah straits as international waterways.

This treaty led both Egyptian President Anwar Sadat and Israeli Prime Minister Menachem Begin to share the 1978 Nobel Peace Prize. However, the Arab nations, and especially the Palestinians, condemned it. Anwar Sadat became unpopular in the Arab world as well as within his own country. This situation led to his assassination on October 6, 1981, by members of the Egyptian Islamic Jihad.[59]

### Draft of Israeli-Lebanese Treaty

During the 1982 Operation Peace for Galilee, the Israeli invasion of Lebanon led to U.S. mediation and pressure. Israel and Lebanon held more than 35 meetings over a year-and-a-half period, resulting in the May 17 Peace Treaty Agreement in 1983.

The negotiating teams were headed by Antoine Fattal for Lebanon and David Kimche for Israel. The treaty called for a staged Israeli (and Syrian) withdrawal over the next eight to twelve weeks and the establishment of a "security zone" to be patrolled by the Lebanese army in southern Lebanon, but was conditional on Syrian withdrawal as well.

In August 1983, as Israel withdrew from the areas southeast of Beirut to the Awali River, Lebanese factions clashed for control of the freed territory.[60] The treaty was never ratified.

### Israeli Peace Proposal

On May 14, 1989, Israel Prime Minister Yitzhak Shamir and Yitzhak Rabin proposed a peace initiative offered by Israel based on Camp David Accords. The proposal was to strengthen the peace with Egypt; to attain peace with other Arab states; to improve conditions for Arab refugees; and to allow elections and self-rule for Palestinian Arabs.

However, these proposals failed because Israel refused to recognize the PLO as a party to any negotiations.

### The Madrid Conference

The Madrid Conference was hosted by the government of Spain and cosponsored by the U.S. and the U.S.S.R. It convened on October 30, 1991, and lasted for three days.

In this conference participated Spain Prime Minister Felipe Gonzalez, U.S.S.R. President Mikhail Gorbachev, Foreign Minister Boris Pankin, President George Bush, Secretary of State James Baker, the Netherland's Foreign Affairs Minister Hans van den Broek for the European Community, and delegations from Egypt, Israel, Jordan, the PLO, Lebanon, and Syria.

It was an early attempt by the international community to start a peace process through negotiations involving Israel and the Palestinian as well as Arab countries, including Syria, Lebanon, and Jordan.[61]

The Madrid Conference initiated a process of one-on-one talks between Israel and each of its Arab neighbors. The U.S. State Department later hosted over a dozen formal sessions between Israel and Jordan, Israel and the Palestinians, Israel and Syria, and Israel and Lebanon.

### The Oslo Accords

The negotiations for the Oslo Accords officially called "Declaration of Principles on Interim Self-Government Arrangements or Declaration of Principles" began secretly in Oslo, Norway, on August 20, 1993. These accords were subsequently officially signed at a public ceremony in Washington, D.C., on September 13, 1993, by Mahmoud Abbas, representing the PLO, and Shimon Peres for Israel. It was witnessed by Israel Prime Minister Yitzhak Rabin, PLO Chairman Yasser Arafat, President Bill Clinton, Secretary of State Warren Christopher, and Russia Foreign Minister Andrei Kozyrev.

As result of this agreement, Israel would withdraw from the Gaza Strip and Jericho. Self-government would be granted to the Palestinians, in stages, for a five-year interim period, which a permanent agreement would be negotiated (beginning no later than May 1996).

It was anticipated that this arrangement would last. Permanent issues, such as positions on Jerusalem, Palestinian refugees, Israeli settlements, security, and borders were deliberately left to be decided at a later stage.

There would be economic cooperation in resources, transportation, and commerce. The West Bank and Jerusalem would be decided later.

Israel and the PLO agreed to recognize each other's right to exist.

The outcome: The Oslo Agreement never succeeded because the PLO never stopped its terrorism, nor did they change their charter to recognize Israel's existence.[62]

The Protocol on Economic Relations concerning Israeli-Palestinian economic cooperation was signed in Paris on February 29, 1994. It was an agreement between Israel and the Palestinian Authority.

*The Israel-Jordan Peace Treaty*

In July 1994, the prime minister of Jordan, Abdelsalam al-Majali, declared an "end to the age of wars," and Israel Foreign Affairs Minister Shimon Peres declared that "the moment of peace has arrived." Rabin and King Hussein held a public meeting with President Clinton at the White House.

On July 25, 1994, Jordan's King Hussein, Israel's Prime Minister Yitzhak Rabin, and President Bill Clinton signed the Washington Declaration in Washington, D.C. This declaration states that Israel and Jordan would end the official state of enmity and would start negotiations in order to achieve an "end to bloodshed and sorrow" and a just and lasting peace.

Once the Palestinian-Israeli talks were progressing, Jordan's King Hussein and Israel's Prime Minister Yitzhak Rabin agreed on a peace treaty. The Israel-Jordan Treaty of Peace was signed by the Israel Prime Minister Rabin and Jordan Prime Minister Abdelsalam al-Majali at the Arabah valley of Israel, near the Jordanian border on October 26, 1994.

It was witnessed by President Bill Clinton and Secretary of State Warren Christopher and made Jordan the second Arab country, after Egypt, to normalize relations with Israel.[63]

*Cairo Agreements on Gaza and Jericho*

On May 4, 1994, PLO Chairman Yasser Arafat and Israel Prime Minister Yitzhak Rabin signed a peace accord called the Agreement on the Gaza Strip and the Jericho Area to apply the Declaration of Principles, especially in Gaza and Jericho.[64] It resulted in a phased transfer of governmental authority to the Palestinians. Much of the Strip (except for the settlement blocs and military areas) came under Palestinian control.

The Israeli forces left Gaza City and other urban areas, leaving the new Palestinian Authority to administer and police the Strip. The Palestinian Authority, led by Yasser Arafat, chose Gaza City as its first provincial headquarters.

## The Jerusalem Embassy Act

On October 23, 1995, the U.S. Congress voted to move the U.S. embassy in Israel from Tel Aviv to Jerusalem and to recognize Jerusalem as the capital of Israel. It resulted in the Embassy Act of 1995. The embassy has yet to be relocated because of stalling on the part of Presidents Clinton and Bush Jr.

## The Oslo Interim Agreement

The elections for the president of the Palestinian National Authority and members of the Palestinian Legislative Council took place on January 20, 1996, following one of the principles of the Interim Agreement that called for Palestinians to hold elections and set up the Palestinian Authority to negotiate a final settlement with Israel.

## The Beilin Abu-Mazen Agreement

The Framework for the Conclusion of a Final Status Agreement Between Israel and the PLO, better known as the Abu-Mazen Agreement, was negotiated for a year and a half by Israel Minister of Economy and Planning Yossi Beilin and Secretary of the Executive Committee of the Fatah Movement Abu Mazen (Mahmoud Abbas) and finally drafted on October 31, 1995.

This agreement was never ratified. Its existence was denied even for five years before being published in September 2000. Although both sides rejected it, the agreement's principles showed up in later negotiations.

## The Oslo II Agreement

The Interim Agreement on the West Bank and the Gaza Strip or Israeli-Palestinian Interim Agreement, or simply the Interim Agreement, also known as Oslo II, was an agreement about the future of the Gaza Strip and extending autonomy to the West Bank.

It was first signed in Taba in the Sinai Peninsula by Israel and the PLO on September 24, 1995, and then four days later on September 28, 1995, by Israeli Prime Minister Yitzhak Rabin and PLO Chairman Yasser Arafat and witnessed in Washington, D.C., by President Bill Clinton as well as by representatives of Russia, Egypt, Jordan, Norway, and the E.U.

## The Grapes of Wrath Understanding

Operation Grapes of Wrath was a 16-day military blitz against Lebanon that started on April 11, 1996. Israeli aircraft and artillery began an intensive bombardment of southern Lebanon as well as targets in the Beirut area and in the Bekaa Valley.

The declared objective of these attacks was to put pressure on the government of Lebanon so that it would curb the activities of Hezbollah in an attempt to retaliate for Hezbollah's bombing of northern Israel. Israel conducted more than 1,100 air raids and extensive shelling (some 25,132 shells). A U.N. installation was also hit by Israeli shelling, causing the death of 118 Lebanese civilians.

More than 600 Hezbollah cross-border rocket attacks targeted northern Israel, particularly the town of Kiryat Shmona. Hezbollah forces also participated in numerous engagements with Israeli and south Lebanon army forces. The conflict was de-escalated on April 27 by a cease-fire agreement banning attacks on civilians.[65]

## The Hebron Accord

The Protocol Concerning the Redeployment in Hebron, also known as the Hebron Agreement, began on January 7, 1997, and was concluded on January 15, 1997. It was signed at the Erez Checkpoint by Israel Prime

Minister Benjamin Netanyahu and PLO Chairman Yasser Arafat, under the supervision of Secretary of State Warren Christopher.

It was concerned about sovereignty over Hebron and aimed to the redeployment of Israeli military forces in Hebron in accordance with the Interim Agreement on the West Bank and the Gaza Strip (Oslo II) of September 1995. The result of this accord was an Israeli Defense Forces withdrawal of 80 percent of Hebron within 10 days. By March 7, 1997, Israel would begin the first phase of withdrawal from rural areas in the West Bank.

Eight months after the first stage, Israel would carry out the second phase of the withdrawal. The third phase was to have been completed before mid-1998. In this phase Israel would withdraw from the remaining parts of the West Bank apart from "settlements and military locations."[66]

### Letter of Assurance from PLO Chairman Yasser Arafat

On January 13, 1998, Yasser Arafat, PLO chairman and president of Palestine, sent a letter to President Bill Clinton assuring the U.S. that the provisions in the PLO charter calling for the destruction of Israel were null and void. (At the same time Arafat made speeches to his people in Arabic telling his people that he never intended to void them!)

### The Wye Memorandum

The Wye River Memorandum was an agreement negotiated between Israel and the Palestine Authority to implement the earlier Interim Agreement of September 28, 1995. Brokered by the U.S. at the Aspen Institute Wye River Conference Center, it was signed on October 23, 1998, by President Bill Clinton, Israel Prime Minister Benjamin Netanyahu, PLO Chairman Yasser Arafat, and Jordan King Hussein.

Clinton opened the summit at the secluded Wye River Conference Center on October 15 and returned at least six times to the site to press Netanyahu and Arafat to finalize the deal. In the final push to get Netanyahu and Arafat to overcome remaining obstacles, Clinton invited

King Hussein, who had played a past role in easing tensions between the two men, to join the talks.

Israel agreed to a staged withdrawal from 13 percent of its "occupied" territory. The Palestinians agreed to suppress terror and get rid of their stockpiled weapons, to take steps to stop inciting violence, and to stop the hate-filled anti-Israel propaganda.

As results of this accord, Israel withdrew from some of the territories, while the Palestinian cracked down on militants and opened the Palestinian National Airport. However, the Palestinians did not disarm or stop brainwashing their citizens. Therefore, Israel stopped their withdrawals.

On November 17, 1998, Israel's 120-member parliament, the Knesset, approved the Wye River Memorandum by a vote of 75–19.[67]

The Wye meetings were marked by heavy pressure on Israel's Prime Minister Netanyahu, highlighted by the emotional speech by King Hussein of Jordan, who was dying of brain cancer. Netanyahu had always been against land for peace. It must have taken extreme intimidation by the delegation, especially by President Clinton, to change his stance.

Afterward, Netanyahu lost the confidence of the people of Israel. Some thought he gave away too much, while some felt it was too little. On television news, he looked like a beaten, broken man. He was voted out of office a few months later.

### The Opening of Final Status Negotiations

The Opening of Negotiations on the Framework Agreement on Permanent Status between Israel and the Palestinians started on November 8, 1999, in the West Bank city of Ramallah. These negotiations took place to determine the final status of the peace agreement and were led by Israel Prime Minister Ehud Barak and PLO Chairman Yasser Arafat, under the supervision of Secretary of State Madeleine Albright.

It was a follow-up on the Wye agreements, but the negotiations never arrived to a point of agreement. The interim process put in place under Oslo had fulfilled neither Israeli nor Palestinian expectations.

## The Camp David Summit Statement

The Middle East Peace Summit at Camp David of July 2000 took place at the Naval Support Facility Thurmont, popularly known as Camp David in Maryland. These negotiations were leaded by President Bill Clinton, Israeli Prime Minister Ehud Barak, and PLO Chairman Yasser Arafat. It was an ultimately unsuccessful attempt to negotiate a "final status settlement" to the Israeli-Palestinian conflict.

On July 11, the Camp David 2000 Summit convened. The summit ended on July 25, without an agreement being reached. At its conclusion, a Trilateral Statement was issued defining the agreed principles to guide future negotiations.

Another attempt to come up with a final status agreement; no agreement was made.

## The Sharm el-Sheikh Conference 2000

On October 17, 2000, President Bill Clinton met with Middle Eastern leaders for two days in Sharm el-Sheikh, Egypt, in a U.S.-sponsored attempt to deliver security for both sides—lightening Israeli restrictions on Arabs in Israel and ending the violence.

The host of the negotiations was Egyptian President Hosni Mubarak. The leaders involved were Israel Prime Minister Ehud Barak and PLO Chairman Yasser Arafat. As a result of these negotiations, a U.S.-led commission issued the Mitchell Report, which recommended more negotiations, an end to violence on both sides, and a freeze on Israeli settlements in contested areas.

Four days later, the Arab League met in Cairo, Egypt, with Mubarak hosting. All parties praised the intifada (the holy war or "jihad") against Israel. Once again, the Arab leaders said one thing at the summit and another thing among themselves. After the Sharm el-Sheikh Conference, the Al-Aqsa Intifada went on as before.

## The Clinton Bridging Proposals

In December 2000, President Clinton wrote up a summary of the issues and offered it to both sides. It seemed to be accepted, but it came to nothing.

## Tenet Plan

Following the failure of the Mitchell Plan to end the Palestinian-Israeli violence begun in September 2000, CIA Director George Tenet offered a plan to cease violence and resume negotiations, provided there would be one week without violence. The plan was supposed to begin in June 2001, but there was never a violence-free week! On September 11, 2001, President Bush issued drafts of a speech to the State Department for their review; it was later reported that President Bush had been prepared to announce his support for a Palestinian state prior to the September 11 terrorist attacks on Washington, D.C. and New York City.

State Department and other senior administration officials told CNN that drafts of a major policy speech on the Middle East, to be delivered by Secretary of State Powell, had been circulating within the State Department for review. The speech was to "clarify its [U.S.] views on an end result" of the (Mideast) peace process, which would lead to the eventual "creation of a Palestinian state."[68]

Powell had expected to deliver the speech on the sidelines of the U.N. General Assembly that began on September 23, but that plan was put on hold after the September 11 terrorist attacks on the World Trade Center and Pentagon. A future address to the U.N. was postponed because security couldn't be guaranteed for U.N. members. The timing of the terrorist attacks was not just a coincidence.

The greatest attack ever on American soil occurred. The hijacking of four airplanes and the attack on the World Trade Center and the Pentagon left approximately 3,500 dead and thousands injured. These suicide attacks by Muslim terrorists caused over $100 billion dollars in damage and financial losses and stunned the country.

The attack was aimed directly at the financial heart of the U.S. The effect of this attack on the stock market was devastating. The week after the attack was one of the worst ever for the stock market—a catalyst for an economic depression that could affect the entire world.

### *The Arab Peace Initiative (Saudi Peace Plan)*

In March 2002, at an Arab League summit conference in Beirut, Lebanon, Saudi Crown Prince Abdullah proposed an Arab peace plan, calling for Israel to withdraw from all territories it won since 1967 and for the right of the Palestine refugees to return to Israel in return for Arab recognition of Israel and peaceful relations. Absent were Jordan's king and Egypt's president. Palestinian Chairman Yasser Arafat was trapped by Israel in his office in Ramallah.

### *Jerusalem: The Foreign Relations Authorization Act*

On September 30, 2002, the U.S. Congress called for a clearer recognition of Jerusalem as Israel's capital with the Foreign Relations Authorization Act (H.R. 1646), signed by President George W. Bush that included the following provisions (Sec. 214, 215): The Congress maintains its commitment to relocating the U.S. Embassy in Israel to Jerusalem and urges the president, pursuant to the Jerusalem Embassy Act of 1995, to immediately begin the process of relocating the U.S. Embassy in Israel to Jerusalem.

President Bush ignored this act as had President Clinton. The embassy remains in Tel Aviv.

### *The Quartet and the Road Map*

The Road Map for peace was a plan to resolve the Israeli-Palestinian conflict proposed by a quartet of international entities—the U.S., the E.U., Russia, and the U.N.—that started meet on June 24, 2002.

The members of the quartet were trying to mediate a multi-step plan called the Road Map, which was championed by President George W. Bush. The steps and the penalties for breaking the agreement were very vague. The Road Map still looms over Israel, but has not yet been traveled on because the Palestinians have never let up the violence.

The Road Map negotiated between Israel Prime Minister Ariel Sharon and Palestine Prime Minister Mahmoud Abbas comprised three goal-driven phases with the ultimate goal of ending the conflict as early as 2005. The steps of the Road Map were:

*Phase I* (as early as May 2003): End to Palestinian violence; Palestinian political reform; Israeli withdrawal to the borders of September 2000 and from West Bank Palestinian cities and freeze on settlement expansion; and the Palestinians would hold democratic elections.

*Phase II* (as early as June–December 2003): International conference to support Palestinian economic recovery and launch a process, leading to establishment of an independent Palestinian state.

*Phase III* (as early as 2004–2005): Second international conference; permanent status agreement and end of conflict; agreement on final borders; Israel would return to its 1967 borders (without East Jerusalem!), refugees and settlements; Arab state to agree to peace deals with Israel.

## Sharm el-Sheikh Conference 2005

The Sharm el-Sheikh Conference took place on February 8, 2005, where Israel Prime Minister Ariel Sharon, Palestine Authority President Mahmoud Abbas, Egypt President Hosni Mubarak, and King Abdullah II of Jordan met in an effort to put an end to the four-year Al-Aqsa Intifada.

The agreements reached aimed that in exchange for an end to PLO violence, Israel would release 900 Palestinian prisoners and withdraw from several cities. Besides, Egypt and Jordan would send ambassadors back to Israel and the Intifada was declared to be over!

Results: Whoops! As usual, the Palestinians broke the newly established peace with a suicide bombing in Tel Aviv.

## Sharon's Disengagement Plan

The Disengagement Plan Implementation Law, also known as the Disengagement Plan or Gaza Expulsion Plan, was a proposal by Israel Prime Minister Ariel Sharon, adopted by the Knesset and Israel government on June 6, 2004, and enacted in August 2005, to evict all Israelis from the Gaza Strip and from four settlements in the northern West Bank.

This law commanded all the civilians to withdraw from the Gaza Strip and four settlements in the northern West Bank. The settlements would also remain standing so that the Palestinians could take them over and Israel would patrol the border between Egypt and Gaza. The Palestinian airport and the port in Dahanieh would remain closed, but the Erez joint industrial area would remain in business. Finally, the borders were not final until the Palestinians fulfill their agreement to control terrorism.

Those Israeli citizens who refused to accept government compensation packages and voluntarily vacate their homes prior to the August 15, 2005 deadline were evicted by Israeli security forces over a period of several days. The eviction of all residents, demolition of the residential buildings, and evacuation of associated security personnel from the Gaza Strip was completed by September 12, 2005. The eviction and dismantlement of the four settlements in the northern West Bank was completed 10 days later.

For the first time, the Israeli army was ordered to use force against their own citizens. Eight thousand residents were evacuated from their homes. They were promised to be relocated and paid by the government for their houses. Most have never received a single cent, and for over a year many lived in tent cities or with relatives.

As soon as the Israelis were gone, all the terrorist groups moved in with their weapons. Attacks into Israel started right away.

*Olmert's New Borders for Israel*

In March 2006, Israeli Prime Minister Ehud Olmert proposed giving away large areas of Israel, including the West Bank and East Jerusalem. He didn't want to protect areas with an Arab majority. Most of Israel agreed with him.

On May 30, 2006, Egyptian President Hosni Mubarak voiced his objection to Israel's plan to give up the West Bank. He feared Hamas terrorism against Israel would spread into Egypt!

# 11

# *The Saga of* Jonathan Pollard

I s the U.S. holding a dangerous criminal in prison for life, or have we used him as a pawn to double-cross Israel?

Jonathan Pollard is serving a life sentence without parole for passing intelligence documents to Israel. Is this a political travesty of justice, or is he getting what he deserves?

According to his own website (www.jonathanpollard.org), Pollard is one of the most mistreated and double-crossed American heroes in history. According to U.S. defense and intelligence agencies, Pollard is one of the most treasonous and dangerous men in history.

In the 1980s, Jonathan Pollard worked for the U.S. navy as an intelligence analyst. He discovered that information vital to Israel was being withheld by our government. He found intelligence reports about weapons of mass destruction being developed by Syria, Iraq, Libya, and Iran. There were nuclear, chemical, and biological weapons with ballistic missiles that could deliver them to civilian areas of Israel.

According to his website, Pollard tried to convince his superiors to share these reports with Israel, so Israel could better protect itself from Arab unconventional attacks. He was told to forget about it. Apparently, the U.S. government wanted to keep Israel, a close ally, from defending itself!

As a Jewish American, Pollard's concern for Israel's safety prompted him to take matters into his own hands and pass the reports to Israel himself. He delivered briefcases of classified documents to Israel until he was found out in 1985. On advice from Israel, Pollard sought refuge in the Israeli embassy in Washington but was refused sanctuary. He was arrested outside the building by the FBI.

## THE TRIAL AND SENTENCE

Pollard and his attorneys were not allowed to see evidence presented by Defense Secretary Caspar Weinberger. One memo was shown to them right before his sentencing, when no defense could be made. The memo accused Pollard of treason. Treason does not apply when dealing with a friendly nation. Because no one was shown the memos, rumors and innuendoes spread and became accepted as fact. He was accused of passing huge volumes of documents to Israel, which he says was exaggerated a thousandfold.

The U.S. attorney arranged a plea bargain with Pollard: He would plead guilty to the one count of passing classified information to an ally without intent to harm the U.S. There would be no trial, and no risk of classified information being disclosed in court. In return, the government said it would not seek the maximum sentence. Therefore, he cooperated with investigators and was promised leniency in return. The trial judge warned Pollard, however, that he could still receive a life sentence. Pollard nevertheless pled guilty on June 4, 1986.

In spite of there being no trial, no indictment for treason or harming the U.S., Pollard was sentenced to life in prison without parole!

Spies are executed or imprisoned for life when they spy for an enemy nation at war with us, but we were never at war with Israel! Why was his sentence so excessive?

A life sentence was the heaviest penalty in history for a spy working for an ally. The usual sentence is two to four years, with possible parole, but agent Ron Olive, the agent who caught Pollard, says this is untrue and notes that "espionage statutes do not differentiate between adversaries and allies." He also makes the more questionable claim that "no one in the history of the U.S. who spied for an ally or adversary came close to causing the colossal damage Pollard did to our national security."

Alan Dershowitz argued that Pollard's sentence was far greater than the average term imposed for spying for the Soviet Union and other enemies of the U.S. Still, many convicted spies have been given life sentences, including Aldrich Ames, Robert Hanssen, and John Walker.

Pollard's original attorneys never appealed. Could the government have gotten to them? Every challenge and appeal filed later with new attorneys was rejected.

Pollard's wife, Anne, served a five-year sentence for unauthorized possession of government documents. She divorced her husband after her release.

At first, Israel denied using anyone to spy on the U.S. In 1998, the government of Benjamin Netanyahu admitted that Pollard had worked for Israeli intelligence and granted him citizenship. Netanyahu requested clemency for Pollard during Middle East peace talks at the Wye Plantation in Maryland in 1998.

Israeli requests for Pollard's release really began with Prime Minister Yitzhak Rabin in 1995. The next prime minister, Shimon Peres, proposed a spy swap with the Palestinians. President Clinton promised to release Pollard as part of a peace agreement, but after Rabin was killed, Clinton dropped the issue.

## WYE: THE PROMISE, THE BETRAYAL

Israeli Prime Minister Benjamin Netanyahu was reluctant to join the Wye peace talks in 1998 (see "The Peace Process" chapter). To entice him, Clinton offered the carrot of Pollard's release if Netanyahu would come. After days of manipulation and pressure on peace issues, a bitter Netanyahu was about to walk out on the talks when Clinton promised Pollard's release. Netanyahu agreed to sign the accords. Just before the signing, with the press cameras rolling, Clinton denied that he had ever made that offer. Netanyahu lost his credibility at home, leading to defeat in the Israeli elections. (Israel can call for elections anytime the public is unhappy with its leadership.)

The U.S. pushed for the release of Palestinian prisoners held in Israel, promising to release Pollard. The deal was: one man in exchange for 750 known murderers. The Wye summit ended with Israel releasing the prisoners in exchange for nothing. The terrorists continued to plan and stage deadly attacks against Israeli civilians.

Pollard's supporters in the U.S. also routinely request that he be pardoned. President Clinton reportedly considered a pardon, but defense and intelligence agency officials have vigorously opposed the idea. At the end of Clinton's term, the issue was again raised and Sen. Richard Shelby, chairman of the Senate's Select Committee on Intelligence, along with a majority of senators argued against a pardon. "Mr. Pollard is a convicted spy who put our national security at risk and endangered the lives of our intelligence officers," Shelby said. "There are not terms strong enough to express my belief that Mr. Pollard should serve every minute of his sentence."

James Woolsey, former head of the CIA, has confirmed this was "a serious espionage case," but said it was not true that the information given to Pollard was leaked to other countries. He said the main issue was the U.S. fear that Israel's intelligence services might be penetrated by enemies who then could access the material Pollard passed on. Woolsey also contradicted claims that Pollard only passed information that was relevant to Israel's security. "As for the quality of the information, in my opinion, at the time [1993] the material was broad-ranging and included information that did not relate solely to Israel's immediate security needs. Part of it, if it had found its way into the hands of a hostile country, would have presented a danger to the U.S. ability to collect intelligence."

In 2001, Rabbi Steven Pruzansky of New Jersey met with Netanyahu. The former prime minister described President Clinton as "very hostile to Israel, clearly a friend of the Palestinians." Netanyahu simply ended: "Clinton lied to me. Now that's a shocking disclosure."[69]

## GOOD GUY OR BAD GUY?

Opinions differ on Pollard as a good or bad guy, especially within the U.S. government.

Before sentencing, and in violation of the plea agreement, Pollard and his wife broke terms of his plea agreement by speaking repeatedly to the press. They bragged about spying and tried to gain the sympathies of Jewish people in the U.S.

They both appeared on *60 Minutes*. Anne Pollard declared, "I feel my husband and I did what we were expected to do, and what our moral obligation was as Jews, what our moral obligation was as human beings, and I have no regrets about that."

Also prior to sentencing, Secretary of Defense Caspar Weinberger submitted a 46-page classified memorandum to the judge, outlining the damage to U.S. national security done by Pollard.

Wolf Blitzer interviewed Pollard in jail three weeks before sentencing and wrote an article for the *Washington Post* called "Pollard: Not a Bumbler, but Israel's Master Spy." Pollard related details that he had given Israel, revealing classified information about capabilities and defenses of the PLO, Libya, and many other Arab countries, both friends and foes.[70]

Contrary to some accounts, Blitzer reported that Pollard and his attorneys were permitted to read it and draft a response. Weinberger called for severe punishment, and the memo is widely cited as a major reason that the judge ultimately sentenced Pollard to life in prison for espionage.

The breaking of the plea agreement in which Pollard swore not to disclose classified material he obtained while working for the navy and swore not to "provide information for purposes of publication or dissemination" unless it was reviewed by the director of naval intelligence remain one possible reason for Pollard to remain in prison despite a change in U.S. parole laws.

## PBS *NOVA*

Incriminating details came from the PBS *Nova* show in 2002. The show claimed that Pollard always imagined himself to be a spy. When he was a student at Stanford University, he made up stories about having contacts in Israeli intelligence and about his father being a CIA agent in Czechoslovakia. He did quirky things, such as filling out school and job applications with fictional names, then mailing himself telegrams addressed to those names.

Was the navy negligent in their background check of Pollard, or did the show make up these allegations?

Early in Pollard's career he lost his high level security clearance due to his suspicious dealings with an attaché from the South African embassy. The show gave no details, and there was never an investigation by the navy. If true, why did Pollard get reinstated and promoted in 1984 to analyst in the Naval Criminal Investigation Service (NCIS)?

The show quotes three coworkers who claim that Pollard soon began mailing them classified information. They had not requested it, nor did they know why he sent it to them. Why didn't the navy do anything if this was true?

Soon after that, Pollard connected with a young Israeli agent named Avi Sella, who requested any information Pollard could give him and offered to pay for it. Pollard gave him details on chemical weapon plants in Iraq. Pollard was paid handsomely then and on a continuing basis. Three times a week for a year, he passed computer printouts, satellite photographs, and classified documents to Sella, who copied and returned them, Pollard was rewarded with a generous salary, lavish gifts for him and his wife, and trips, including a luxury honeymoon aboard the Orient Express.

*Nova* investigators claimed that Pollard admitted passing over 800 classified documents and more than 1,000 cables, which would be the largest amount of information ever passed by a spy. His website refutes that, saying that the government grossly exaggerated the amount of material given to Israel.

In 1993, Secretary of Defense Les Aspin reported that Pollard had tried 14 times to disclose classified information in letters written to various recipients from his prison cell.

## THE MYSTERY REMAINS

The question remains: Is Pollard a hero who saved Israel from harm? Or is he a pathetic nut job who played games of being a spy?

Did he pass information that endangered U.S. security or that of any other country? Or was he falsely accused and smeared with false news reports?

Were the allegations in the press true? Or has the government used Pollard for its purposes for the past years?

If Pollard is such a dangerous criminal, why does Israel want him released so badly that they were willing to trade multiple terrorists for this one man?

Why does the U.S. continue to refuse to release Pollard while pressuring Israel to release their prisoners who are known terrorists, even masterminds of terrorist attacks? Many of those freed Palestinian terrorists continue to attack Israeli citizens!

Who will Pollard hurt if released? Maybe the veracity of the U.S. government?

Pollard denied spying "against" the U.S. He said he provided only information he believed was vital to Israeli security and was being withheld by the Pentagon. This included data on Soviet arms shipments to Syria, Iraqi and Syrian chemical weapons, the Pakistani atomic bomb project, and Libyan air defense systems. Because the information he took is classified, we can't verify if this is true.

In 2006, Rafael Eitan said, "It is likely that we could have gotten the same information without him." He also said, however, that Pollard provided "information of such high quality and accuracy, so good and so important to the country's security" that "my desire, my appetite to get more and more material overcame me." He added that the information might have made a difference had Israel been involved in another war. Eitan also maintained that Pollard never exposed any American agents and that another spy, Aldrich Ames, tried to blame Pollard to divert suspicion from his activities.

The agent in charge of counterintelligence for the NCIS who caught Pollard has said that he was involved in illegal activities to help countries besides Israel. Ron Olive wrote that Pollard confessed that before he spied for Israel, he passed classified information to South Africa, his civilian financial advisers, and a member of the Australian Royal Navy. He also admitted passing documents to Pakistan "in the hopes it would take him on as a spy." Olive quotes Pollard during a debriefing after he pleaded guilty saying, "If I could see it, and touch it, you can assume I got it…. My only limitation was what I couldn't carry." Olive said Pollard stole 360 cubic feet of classified secrets and confessed to stealing classified information two to three times a day, three to four days a week.

## 12

# *The Key Roles of* Three American Presidents

W hile I have integrated numerous modern-day American presidents into various chapters, three are of particular importance as regards the Jewish people and nation: Franklin Delano Roosevelt, Harry Truman, and Lyndon Johnson.

## PRESIDENT ROOSEVELT

During the 1940s, could Franklin Delano Roosevelt have done more to rescue the Jews from the Holocaust? Did he ignore their plight due to the anti-Semitism of the upper class, to which he belonged? Did he allow them to be slaughtered, or was fighting the war and winning it the only means of rescue?

His critics maintained that one strong statement from Roosevelt, exposing the evil deeds of the Nazis, might have kept Hitler in check. No such statement was issued.

On the other hand, Roosevelt tried to work with world leaders, including Saudi Arabia's Ibn Saud and Russia's Joseph Stalin, to help Jews escape from the Nazis. In 1938, Roosevelt issued many visas for Jewish refugees. He invited world leaders to a conference in France to discuss putting pressure on Hitler to release Jewish people. His efforts were fruitless, with Britain's Prime Minister Neville Chamberlain retorting, "Use your own embassy for such purposes!"

So what happened with the *St. Louis* in 1939? It was a ship filled with 900 Jewish refugees, sailing first to Cuba and then up and down the U.S. and Canadian coastline, looking for asylum. After Cuba refused to allow them in, the ship sailed to Miami and cabled President Roosevelt for permission to land. The president never answered them. The *St. Louis* was forced to return to Europe, where over 250 of its passengers eventually died in concentration camps.

First Lady Eleanor Roosevelt was more responsive. There was a second refugee ship whose story remained untold for 67 years. On July 8, 2007, the *New York Times* published an article about the *Quanza*, a Portuguese ship carrying 86 Jewish refugees in 1940. They were being refused entry and were ready to turn back when the captain wired Eleanor Roosevelt about their plight. Against the will of Secretary of State Cordell Hull, she quietly issued visas and allowed them all into the U.S.

People close to FDR knew how disturbed he was by the reports of Nazi atrocities in Europe. He tried in vain to negotiate with Germany for the release of 10,000 Jews. In 1942, he submitted the War Powers Bill to suspend immigration quotas. He wanted to help, but he was hamstrung by Congress and the American people!

An immigration quota was passed in 1924, limiting immigration from each country. Eastern Europeans could make up no more than 3 percent of the U.S. population. As Nazi persecution increased, Congress repeatedly voted not to increase the quota. At the time that refuge was most desperately needed, the U.S. slammed its doors in Jewish faces. Waves of Jewish immigrants during the late 1800s and early 1900s had left many Americans anti-Semitic. Still stinging from the Depression, people did not want millions of new Jewish immigrants competing with them for jobs. As strong a president as Roosevelt was, he could not violate immigration law. Secretary Hull hovered close by to enforce it!

Between 1920 and 1921, almost 120,000 Jews came to the U.S. Immigration slowed until 1933 to 1940, when 105,000 Jewish refugees were admitted. We welcomed more Jewish refugees than any other country!

During World War II, FDR tried to convince King Ibn Saud of Saudi Arabia to support Jewish settlement in Palestine. The king refused. Doing a 180° turn, Roosevelt wrote a controversial letter to the king, pledging that the U.S. would not attack any Arab country, and that the U.S. would make no policy change toward Israel without first consulting with the Arab leaders.

In David S. Wyman's book, *The Abandonment of the Jews: America and the Holocaust, 1941–1945*, he examines allegations that officials in the Roosevelt administration knew, in surprising detail, about Adolf Hitler's plans to exterminate all the Jews in Nazi Europe—and that these officials did little to prevent the massacre. Wyman concludes that senior American officials could indeed have saved many thousands, if not millions, of European Jews by intervening earlier. He suggests that a combination of anti-Semitism and indifference to anything not perceived as being of direct strategic importance to the U.S. indirectly led to countless deaths.

Questions remain as to FDR's real sentiments based on the following:

- Evidence that he knew about the extermination of the Jews by the Nazis as early as 1942.
- Severely limited Jewish immigration into the U.S., only allowing 10 percent of the quota.
- Refused to bomb the gas chambers or the railways leading to the concentration camps. Said he didn't have the resources, but they were transporting troops by the tens of thousands. The U.S. was bombing in Germany less than five miles from Auschwitz.

- Never spoke out against the Nazi Holocaust.
- Never pressured England to allow Jewish immigration into Palestine.
- U.S. War Refugee Board: Too little too late! Not sufficiently staffed or financed! It did help Raoul Wallenberg rescue 200,000 Jews from Hungary who would have gone to the camps.
- He admitted 1,000 Italian refugees into a camp in Oswego, New York. Only 1,000!
- The 900 Jewish refugees from Germany on the *St. Louis* were refused admission to the U.S. in 1939.
- Was anti-Semitism involved partly due to coming elections, and mostly due to wanting to further the interests of U.S. oil companies by pleasing the oil-rich Arab nations, especially Saudi Arabia?

## PRESIDENT TRUMAN

U.S. support for the partition of Palestine was crucial to the adoption of the U.N. partition plan and to the creation of the state of Israel. During World War II, the U.S. was anxious to maintain good relations with Saudi Arabia. President Roosevelt had promised King Saud that the U.S. would make no policy decisions about Palestine without consulting the Arabs, though Roosevelt tried to enlist Saud's support for allowing Jewish immigration to Palestine. Following Roosevelt's verbal promise to Saud to consult the Arabs about Palestine policy, he reiterated the promise in writing on April 5, 1945. However, a week later, Roosevelt was dead, replaced by Vice President Harry S. Truman, and the end of the war created a different political reality as well as bringing the revelation of massive murder of Jews in the Holocaust.

Truman was a friend of the Jewish people, and he gave his support to the Zionist movement before World War II. He had heard about the Nazi atrocities and was even more resolved to help the Jews in any way he could. At a Chicago rally in 1944, then Senator Truman said, "Today, not tomorrow, we must do all that is humanly possible to provide a haven for all those who can be grasped from the hands of Nazi butchers. Free lands must be opened to them."

Truman wrote in his memoirs: "The question of Palestine as a Jewish homeland goes back to the solemn promise that had been made to them [the Jews] by the British in the Balfour Declaration of 1917—a promise which had stirred the hopes and the dreams of these oppressed people. This promise, I felt, should be kept, just as all promises made by responsible, civilized governments should be kept."

After the war, about 250,000 displaced Jewish people were waiting in Europe in terrible reassignment camps. Truman tried to pressure the British to allow some of these to immigrate to Palestine. He also petitioned the U.S. to allow an enlarging of immigration for these refugees, but neither country would agree to his request.

He wrote to Senator Joseph Ball of Minnesota on November 24, 1945: "I told the Jews that if they were willing to furnish me with 500,000 men to carry on a war with the Arabs, we could do what they are suggesting in the Resolution [favoring a state]—otherwise we will have to negotiate awhile. It is a very explosive situation we are facing, and naturally I regret it very much, but I don't think that you, or any of the other senators, would be inclined to send half a dozen divisions to Palestine to maintain a Jewish State. What I am trying to do is to make the whole world safe for the Jews. Therefore, I don't feel like going to war for Palestine."

Truman was convinced by the State Department that the Zionists were communists, and they could become a satellite state for the Russians. And, of course, the concern for foreign oil was always a factor.

A Jewish war buddy and ex-business partner, Eddie Jacobsen, visited Truman at the White House on June 26, 1946, bringing with him some American Zionist officials. According to Henry Wallace, Truman said, "Jesus Christ couldn't please them when he was here on earth, so how can anyone expect that I would have any luck?"

Truman wrote to the king of Saudi Arabia, stating his support for a Jewish Homeland in Palestine and inviting Saud to the U.S. to discuss the question.

In 1947, British soldiers were turning Jewish immigrant ships back and forcing passengers to disembark in Cyprus and hanging Jewish underground members. The U.N. met in special session in April to form a United Nations Special Committee on Palestine (UNSCOP) in May that would come up with a solution for Palestine. The U.S.S.R. was surprisingly no longer opposed to partition.

In July 1947, while UNSCOP was in Palestine, the British turned the *Exodus* immigrant ship back to Europe. Following a nightlong hand-to-hand battle, Jewish immigrants rescued from concentration camps lay on the hot filthy decks in Haifa as reporters and cameras covered the story. When the passengers were ultimately returned to Hamburg, Germany, the cameras and reporters were there again. A vast wave of public sentiment for partition and a Jewish state was generated. In a late 1947 poll, 65 percent of Americans supported partition.

On September 17, 1947, Secretary of State George Marshall, addressing the U.N., indicated that the U.S. was reluctant to endorse the partition of Palestine. However, as the Soviet Union had now come out in favor of partition, Truman, having previously supported it, could certainly not back down at this point.

The State Department now attempted to detach the Negev from the Jewish state. Truman was persuaded by Chaim Weizmann after showing him maps of the area. He was brought to the White House in November by Eddie Jacobson, to support keeping the Negev, about half the area of Israel, in the Jewish state.

The partition resolution required a two-thirds majority to pass, and it became evident that due to Arab pressure and resistance to the U.S. by third-world countries, it might not pass. On November 25, a Tuesday, U.N. General Assembly members, acting as an *ad hoc* committee on Palestine, voted. The partition resolution passed the "committee" vote, 25–13, with 17 abstentions. However, this vote was one short of the majority that would be needed to pass the General Assembly itself.

The vote was postponed from Wednesday, giving the lobbyists Thursday, the Thanksgiving holiday, to change votes. The Arab countries exerted pressure against partition. Pressure from Zionists, U.S. officials, and former officials was brought to bear on countries that were intending to vote against partition. Greece was threatened with loss of foreign aid. Apparently on the prompting of former Secretary of State Stettinus, tire manufacturer Harvey Firestone threatened Liberia with a rubber embargo. Paraguay, the Philippines, Haiti, and other countries reversed their positions and voted for partition. Though newspapers accused State Department officials of acting against partition, at least some State Department officials were directly involved in lobbying for it.

Dean Rusk, head of the State Department's U.N. desk in Washington, D.C., later wrote: "When President Truman decided to support partition, I worked hard to implement it.... The pressure and arm-twisting applied by American and Jewish representatives in capital after capital to get that affirmative vote are hard to describe."

The vote was again postponed to Saturday, November 29, one more day, at the request of the Arabs. Greece voted against partition anyway, but Zionist pressure continued on other countries.

An American Zionist delegation met with Truman in January 1948 at the White House and demanded immediate help for the thousands of homeless Holocaust victims seeking refuge in a Jewish state. Truman's response was not satisfactory, and the visitors became adamant. Rabbi Abba Hillel Silver of Cleveland pounded on the president's desk. Truman was outraged. "No one, but no one, comes into the office of the president of the United States and shouts at him, or pounds on his desk. If anyone is going to do any shouting or pounding in here, it will be me." Truman had them ushered out of the Oval Office and said to his staff. "I've had it with those hotheads. Don't ever admit them again, and what's more, I also never want to hear the word Palestine mentioned again."

Fearful that Truman would waver in U.S. support, American Zionists enlisted Eddie Jacobson to attempt to sway the president to see Weizmann once again, despite his earlier ban on Zionists. Truman at first refused. He wrote on February 27 to Jacobson that he would not learn anything new from Weizmann and added: "The Jews are so emotional, and the Arabs are so difficult to talk with, that it is almost impossible to get anything done. The British have, of course, been exceedingly uncooperative.... The Zionists, of course, have expected a big stick approach on our part, and naturally have been disappointed when we can't do that."

On March 18, 1948, Truman met Weizmann and reassured him of U.S. support for a Jewish state, promising to recognize the state whether or not it was declared under U.N. auspices.

Truman wrote in his diary: "State Department pulled the rug from under me today. I didn't expect that would happen. In Key West or en route there from St. Croix, I approved the speech and statement of policy by Sen. Austin to U.N. meeting. This morning I find that the State Department has reversed my Palestine policy. The first I know about it is what I see in the papers! Isn't that hell! Now, I am placed in a position of a liar and double-crosser. I never felt so in my life....

"There are people on the third and fourth levels of the State Department who have always wanted to cut my throat. They've succeeded in doing so....

"What is not generally understood is that the Zionists are not the only ones to be considered in the Palestine question. There are other interests that come into play, each with its own agenda. The military is concerned with the problems of defending a newly created small country from attacks by much larger and better trained Arab nations. Others have selfish interests concerning the flow of Arab oil to the U.S. Since they all cannot have their way, it is a perfect example of why I had to remember that 'The Buck Stops Here.'"

At a press conference the next day, Truman said, in answer to a question about recognition, "I will cross that bridge when I get to it."

He got to the bridge on May 14, 1948. While the U.N. was still meeting in special session, Clark Clifford got Eliahu Eilat (Epstein), who was representing the Jewish state, to send a note informing the president that a Jewish state had been declared, asking for recognition. Robert Lovett, the deputy Secretary of Defense, informed by Clifford of the president's intentions, asked that the president wait until 10 p.m., when the U.N. would no longer be in session. However, Truman signed the letter of recognition shortly after 6 p.m., giving *de facto* recognition to the new state and its government. In the prepared statement, written before the name of the state was announced, he crossed out the words "Jewish state" and wrote "Israel." Likewise, he inserted the word "provisional" before the word "government."

The real struggle over partition, however, did not take place at the U.N. It took place in the White House. For most members of the Truman Administration there was seemingly little strategic value in supporting the establishment of a fledgling Jewish state. Such a state, it was argued, would be militarily weak and would instantly become economically dependent on the West. The damage that support for such a decision could do to American oil interests in the Gulf would be incalculable. A vigorous campaign to thwart the creation of Israel was therefore launched by the State Department, the Department of Defense, and oil executives. James Forrestal, the Secretary of Defense, augmented his concern for the oil gap by openly portraying Zionist pressure as a scourge. "No group in this country," he told the chairman of the Democratic National Committee, "should be permitted to influence our policy to the point where it could endanger our national security."

From the point of view of the Americans and world opinion, the creation of Israel was a more or less conscious and willful act that was meant to compensate for the Holocaust. This view has been accepted by the Arabs, who protest that the Palestinians should not have been made to pay for the Holocaust. For his part in the drama, Truman is revered by Zionists and hated by Arab partisans.

Yet what Truman understood was that the Jewish people in Palestine and the thousands of refugees still suffering in internment camps would face grave injustice if the long held promise of statehood was not fulfilled.

The idea that Truman had initially entertained, and that the State Department encouraged, that a Jewish state could only be defended by hundreds of thousands of U.S. troops, proved to be groundless. It is probably this realization more than any that truly convinced all and overcame the single greatest objection.

Truman was certainly aware of Arab opposition. The Arab League and the Arab Higher Committee had made clear their opposition to partition both before and after the partition vote, in quite unequivocal terms, and had graphically described exactly what they planned to do to the Jews of Palestine.

The "single state for all" proposed by the Arabs, led by Nazi collaborator Haj Amin al-Husseini, Grand Mufti of Jerusalem, was not likely to be a state where Jews would survive in peace, given that Husseini had told the British that his plan for solving the "Jewish Problem" in Palestine was the same as the one adopted by Nazis in Europe.

At midnight on May 14, 1948, the Provisional Government of Israel proclaimed the new State of Israel. On that same date the U.S., in the person of President Truman, recognized the provisional Jewish government as *de facto* authority of the new Jewish state (de jure recognition was extended on January 31). The U.S. delegates to the U.N. and top ranking State Department officials were angered that Truman released his recognition statement to the press without notifying them first. On May 15, 1948, the Arab states issued their response statement, and Arab armies invaded Israel and the first Arab-Israeli war began.

For his part, Truman once asserted, "Hitler had been murdering Jews right and left. I saw it, and I dream about it even to this day. The Jews needed some place where they could go. It is my attitude that the American government couldn't stand idly by while the victims [of] Hitler's madness are not allowed to build new lives."

President Truman, by granting immediate recognition to Israel, led the world in extending friendship and welcome to a people who have long sought and justly deserve freedom and independence.

In the 1948 Democratic Party Platform, it states: "We pledge full recognition to the State of Israel. We affirm our pride that the United States, under the leadership of President Truman, played a leading role in the adoption of the resolution of November 29, 1947, by the U.N. General Assembly for the creation of a Jewish state. We approve the claims of the State of Israel to the boundaries set forth in the United

Nations' resolution of November 29 and consider that modifications thereof should be made only if fully acceptable to the State of Israel. We look forward to the admission of the State of Israel to the U.N. and its full participation in the international community of nations. We pledge appropriate aid to the State of Israel in developing its economy and resources. We favor the revision of the arms embargo to accord to the State of Israel the right of self-defense. We pledge ourselves to work for the modification of any resolution of the United Nations to the extent that it may prevent any such revision."

Truman's favorite psalm had always been Psalm 137, "By the rivers of Babylon we sat and wept when we remembered Zion" (v. 1). By recognizing Israel, Truman knew he would be forever damned by people who did not want the Jews to have their own state—or who did not want it in Palestine. But as Truman always told himself, the ultimate test of any presidential decision was "not whether it's popular at the time, but whether it's right.... If it's right, make it, and let the popular part take care of itself."

Truman once said that "a weeping man is an abomination." But with his reverence for the Bible and ancient history, Truman was profoundly moved to know he had helped regather the Jews in the Holy Land. Told that an Israeli village had been renamed "Kfar Truman," the stricken president had to cover his face with a handkerchief. Soon the president was proudly comparing himself to the ancient Persian king who had enabled the Jews to return to Zion. During a visit to the Jewish Theological Seminary in New York just after Truman left office, Eddie Jacobson introduced his old friend by saying, "This is the man who helped to create the state of Israel." The ex-president brought Eddie up short: "What do you mean 'helped create'? I am Cyrus! I am Cyrus!"

In the end, Truman recognized Israel for many different reasons. The Jews' display of military strength in Palestine had convinced him that U.S. troops would not be needed to defend them. He feared that letting the Russians recognize Israel first would give them a foothold in Palestine. Truman was also motivated by sheer politics. With a tough campaign ahead, he felt that if he did not recognize Israel, the backers of a Jewish state would make his life a living hell. For the hard-bitten George C. Marshall, Truman's secretary of state, who operated from cold facts on the ground, Israel was chiefly a potential burden for an overstretched U.S. military. But Truman realized helping to found a Jewish state was a historic act that might qualify him for some future edition of "Great Men and Famous Women."

## PRESIDENT JOHNSON

The U.S. tried to prevent the 1967 War through negotiations, but it was not able to persuade Nasser or the other Arab states to cease their belligerent statements and actions. Still, right before the war, President Johnson warned: Israel will not be alone unless it decides to go alone. Then, when the war began, the State Department announced: Our position is neutral in thought, word, and deed.

For some time, the U.S. had an emergency plan to attack Israel. In May 1967, one of the U.S. commands was charged with the task of removing the plan from the safe, refreshing it, and preparing for an order to go into action. However, the preparations lagged behind the developments in the diplomatic arena, and even further behind the successes of Israel's air force and armored divisions in Sinai. The general who was planning to attack Israel made do with extricating frightened American citizens and a panic-stricken ambassador from Jordan.

This unknown aspect of the war was revealed in what was originally a top-secret study conducted by the Institute for Defense Analyses in Washington, D.C. In February 1968, an institute expert, L. Weinstein, wrote an article called "Critical Incident No. 14," about the U.S. involvement in the Middle East crisis of May–June 1967. Only 30 copies of his study were printed for distribution. Years later the material was declassified and can now be read by anyone, although details that are liable to give away sources' identities and operational ideas have remained censored. Strike Command, the entity that was to have launched the attack on Israel, no longer exists.

Even if Johnson had made an unreasonable decision to use his army to block the IDF as it sped to the Suez—contrary to his inclinations, the advice of his aides and what his confidants in the American Jewish community said—he would not have had the requisite military capability. The IDF was faster than the planners, decision makers, and paratroopers of the U.S.

The IDF fought the Egyptians, the Jordanians, and the Syrians without imagining that it might find itself confronting the Americans as well, in their desert camouflage fatigues.[71]

# 13

# *The Peace Process and* Natural Disasters

For decades the U.S. has pressured Israel with the Oslo Accord and the Road Map. God does not take the betrayal of Israel lightly. Every time the U.S. has pressured Israel to give up land, there was a huge natural disaster.

On October 30, 1991, the Madrid Conference began. President George H.W. Bush and Russian President Mikhail Gorbachev met to consider the demands by Syria and the PLO that Israel give up land for peace. At the same time, Hurricane Grace, known as the *Perfect Storm* of movie fame, began to develop in the North Atlantic. The storm traveled 1,000 miles east to west, instead of the usual west to east, sending 35-foot waves, the largest waves ever recorded to crash into the New England coast. The Perfect Storm aimed directly at President Bush's home in Kennebunkport, Maine, causing $1 million in damage.

On August 23, 1992, the Madrid talks moved to Washington, D.C.

On the very first day of the conference, Hurricane Andrew clobbered southern Florida and Louisiana. It was the worst and most expensive storm in U.S. history up to that time, causing damage of $30 billion and leaving 180,000 people homeless in Florida.

From August 20 to September 13, 1993, the Oslo Agreement was in the works. It would be signed on September 13 and finalized with a much-publicized handshake on the White House lawn between President Bill Clinton, Israel's Yitzhak Rabin, and PLO Yasser Arafat. On September 1, during that process, Hurricane Emily pummeled North Carolina with $35 million in damages from floods and extreme high tides.

On January 16, 1994, President Clinton and Syria's President Hafez Al-Assad met in Geneva to discuss another land-for-peace deal, this time about giving up the Golan Heights. The next day the Northridge Earthquake struck. At 6.9 on the Richter scale, Southern California shuddered with the second worst natural disaster in the U.S. at the time, second only to Hurricane Andrew. It was the first earthquake since 1933 to occur in an urban area. Houses fell; streets and overpasses collapsed; gas and water mains broke; more than 2,000 were homeless. It killed 55 people and caused almost $30 billion in damage.

On March 1, 1997, Arafat, whose goal had always been for an independent Palestinian state, arrived in Washington, D.C., to discuss the Har Homa housing project in Israel. The Israeli government had started building 6,500 housing units in East Jerusalem. This housing interfered with Arafat's plans to make Jerusalem the capital of Palestine. The next day he began to speak around the U.S. against Israel.

Also on this day, President Clinton signed a bill into law to fund family planning in 100 countries, and part of those funds was to be used for abortions. That is another issue to bring forth God's retribution on America!

While Arafat toured the country, monstrous tornadoes swept through the nation, hitting Texas, Arkansas, and the Mississippi valley, causing flooding in Ohio and Kentucky. Nearly ten and half inches of rain fell on Louisville, a record. Arkadelphia, Arkansas, was destroyed by the tornados, while flooding devastated Falmouth, Kentucky. On

March 5 and 6, the snowfall in Fargo, North Dakota, reached 99 inches! That record snow melted in April, turning into the worst flooding in a century, accounting for another $1 billion.

On January 21, 1998, President Clinton and Secretary of State Madeleine Albright pressured Israeli Prime Minister Netanyahu to give up land for peace. Meeting at the White House, Clinton and Albright treated him curtly and refused to have lunch with him. Shortly afterward on that day, the Monica Lewinsky scandal broke into the mass media and began to occupy a major portion of Clinton's time. (Okay, so this wasn't a natural disaster, but it was destructive to our nation for other reasons.) Clinton ended up being impeached by Congress, but he never had to leave office.

On September 28, 1998, Clinton met with Arafat and Netanyahu at the White House to talk about giving away land. Later, Arafat addressed the U.N. about declaring an independent Palestinian state by May 1999. The U.N. received him like a hero! The same day, Hurricane George lingered and stalled. Then it strengthened and zeroed in on Key West, Florida, slamming into the Gulf Coast at 110–175 miles per hour, causing major flooding with $1 billion in damage. As soon as Arafat left, the storm dissipated.

From October 15–22, 1998, Arafat and Netanyahu met at the Wye River Plantation in Maryland. The talks were scheduled to last five days with the focus on Israel giving up 13 percent of *Yesha*, the West Bank and Gaza Strip. The talks were extended and concluded on October 23. On October 17, awesome rains and tornadoes hit southern Texas. The San Antonio area was deluged with rain. The rain and flooding in Texas continued until October 22 and then subsided. The floods ravaged 25 percent of Texas and left over $1 billion in damage.

On November 23, 1998, Arafat arrived in Washington again to meet with President Clinton to raise funds for a Palestinian state with Jerusalem as the capital. A total of 42 other nations were represented in Washington, D.C. All the nations agreed to give Arafat $3 billion in aid. Clinton promised $400 million and the European nations $1.7 billion. On the same day, the Dow Jones average dropped 216 points, and on

December 1, the European Market had its third worst day in history. Hundreds of billions of market capitalization were wiped out in the U.S. and Europe.

Arafat`s arrival to U.S. also coincided with a major storm in Oregon, with gusts up to 100 miles per hour on the coast and 50–70 miles per hour elsewhere in Oregon. Power was lost due to downed trees and branches.

A week later, on December 12, Clinton was visiting Palestinian-controlled areas in Israel to discuss the land-for-peace process. He declared that there should be a Palestinian state with Jerusalem as its capital. During his visit, the House of Representatives voted four articles of impeachment against him for lying during the Monica Lewinsky investigation. He was the first president to be impeached in 130 years.

On March 23, 1999, Arafat met with Clinton again in Washington about the Israel land giveaway. Again the Dow Jones average fell 219 points.

On May 3, 1999, the day that Arafat was to declare a Palestinian state, with its capital Jerusalem, the most powerful tornadoes in U.S. history devastated Oklahoma and Kansas with winds of 316 miles per hour, the fastest wind speed ever recorded, causing more than $1 billion in damages.

The declaration was postponed to December 1999 at the request of President Clinton, whose letter to Arafat encouraged him in his aspirations for his own land. He also wrote that the Palestinians have a right to "determine their own future on their own land and that they deserve to live free, today, tomorrow, and forever."

September 13, 1999, the Israeli Foreign Minister and Arafat's deputy worked out a final status deal on Israel's land giveaway. Meanwhile, monster storm Hurricane Floyd slammed the coast of North Carolina coast with 20 inches of rain. Floyd killed 100,000 hogs, 2.47 million chickens, and 500,000 turkeys.

September 21, 1999, Arafat came to Washington, D.C., and visited the U.N. in New York to discuss what became known as the Wye River Memorandum, concerning land for peace. Over the week of October

11, 1999, Israel evicted Jewish settlers from 15 West Bank settlements. As Jewish settlers were evicted from the covenant land in Israel, the Dow Jones financial averages lost 5.7 percent in the worst week since October 1989. On October 15 the Dow lost 266 points and a hurricane slammed into North Carolina. On the next morning, October 16, a magnitude 7.1 earthquake rocked the southwest in the fifth most powerful earthquake in the twentieth century. The earthquake was centered in the California desert and did little damage but was felt in three states.

On January 3–4, 2000, Israeli Prime Minister Ehud Barak agreed to surrender 5 percent of Israel's territory to the Palestinians by the end of that week. On January 25, 2000, the Dow dropped 359 points and the NASDAQ was down 229 points, with over $600 billion in market capitalization wiped out.

On April 12–13, 2000, Barak arrived in Washington, D.C., for talks with Clinton. On April 14, the NASDAQ collapsed, falling over 600 points, experiencing its worst week ever.

On June 16, 2000, Arafat and Clinton met. Clinton sought to culminate a peace agreement by September 13, 2000, which would mark seven years since talks began. The Dow fell 265 points in the final hour of that day.

On July 12, 2000, Barak and Arafat met at Camp David. Talks lasted until July 26, when they ended in disagreement over the Muslim and Jewish sections of the Old City of Jerusalem. During that time, in the western U.S., drought, high winds, and high temperatures sparked some of the worst fires the U.S. had ever seen. Seven million acres were burning in Montana and Wyoming. Dan Glickman, the secretary of agriculture, remarked about the similarity of weather conditions to the Perfect Storm: high winds, high temperatures, lightning, and no rain. Texas suffered its worst drought in history, up to that time.

On May 22, 2001, President George Bush Sr. and Secretary of State Colin Powell supported the Mitchell Report, the summary of the summit at Sharm el-Sheikh, Egypt. The U.S. was to investigate a resolution to the conflict. On May 25, Daniel Kurtzer was nominated to be ambassador to Israel and endorsed by American Jews who favored the land-for-peace plan. On May 26, 2001, Hurricane Adolph struck with peak winds of 145 miles per hour—the strongest hurricane ever in the month of May in the eastern Pacific.

On June 8, CIA director George Tenet along with a special U.S. group hosted talks in Ramallah (Palestinian territory) to restore the current and broken cease-fire. Arafat also met in the West Bank with U.S. Assistant Secretary of State William Burns. Meanwhile, Houston got over two feet of rain overnight, causing terrible flooding. Ten thousand were left homeless, 3,000 homes and businesses were destroyed, and the airport was in chaos from cancelled flights.

On September 1, 2001, Secretary of State Madeleine Albright met with Arab leaders and Israel's Prime Minister Barak. Simultaneously, Hurricane Dennis stalled over the East Coast, and on September 3, Dennis unleashed torrential rains.

On August 17–22, 2005, Israel's Prime Minister Ariel Sharon had been elected based on his promises not only to protect the settlements in the Gaza Strip and the West Bank, but to help them grow. He turned his back on his campaign platform. After 38 years of the people nurturing those lands as part of Israel, Sharon forced the 9,000 residents out of their homes and turned the land over to the Palestinians. The people protested and resisted. The world watched on television as Jewish Israeli soldiers dragged Jewish Israeli citizens from their beautiful middle class neighborhoods and put them on buses to nowhere. People were forced to leave their pets behind to starve to death or be killed by Palestinians. All those beautiful houses were demolished by Israel to please the Palestinians. Many evacuees had the caskets of loved ones moved out of the area so the bodies wouldn't be desecrated. The expelled people were promised money, housing, and help. Most of them got none of those! A year later many were still living in tents or flimsy temporary buildings.

The U.S. was firmly behind the Gaza land-for-peace action, pressuring Israel to go ahead with it. President Bush met with Sharon earlier that month, saying: "I strongly support his courageous initiative to disengage from Gaza and part of the West Bank." On August 29, 2005,

Hurricane Katrina attacked the Gulf Coast. In New Orleans, the levees broke and the city filled up with water. Thousands of people and animals died or became refugees in other states. The news showed crying people torn from their homes and forced to start new lives elsewhere in the U.S. Pets had to be left behind to starve to death or drown. Most houses were demolished by the storm. Caskets uprooted by the floods floated down the streets. Areas in Alabama, Florida, Louisiana, and Texas suffered also.

Israel's Gaza policy was encouraged (no, forcibly imposed!) by the U.S., the E.U., and the U.N. Once "disengagement" was finished, Secretary of State Condoleezza Rice proclaimed, "That's good, but it's just the beginning!" Her meaning: The West Bank and East Jerusalem should be given away next!

On October 17, 2005, hosting his fifth Ishtar dinner at the White House, President Bush praised the spirit and compassion of Islam and thanked our Islamic allies in the coalition in the War on Terror. The president stated, "To promote greater understanding between our cultures, I have encouraged American families to travel abroad, to visit with Muslim families.... And for the first time in our nation's history, we have added a Koran to the White House Library." On October 19, Hurricane Wilma charged into the Mexican island of Cozumel, then into Florida's Gulf Coast on Monday, October 24. The huge storm was nearly 400 miles wide, covering almost the whole state of Florida at one time. Almost half of Key West was under water. Electric power was lost by more customers than by any other natural disaster before it. The storm also set the record for the lowest barometric pressure ever recorded!

*Could all of these incidents be a coincidence? Or is it a God-incidence?*

# 14

# *How Can So Many People* Miss the Connection?

Why do so many of God's people miss the mark about Israel? How can so many genuine born-again, Spirit-filled believers have it so wrong? What were President George W. Bush and Secretary of State Condoleezza Rice thinking? How is that so many churches don't understand the biblical mandate of Genesis 12:2–3:

*I will make you into a great nation and I will bless you; I will make your name great, and you will be a blessing. I will bless those who bless you, and whoever curses you I will curse; and all peoples on earth will be blessed through you.*

People act as though Israel no longer matters to God or to anyone else. Do they think that everything God says in the Bible is just flowery allegories? Do they think that all the promises and blessings now go to the Church? Or do they think that there really are no promises and blessings or curses regarding Israel?

God says He will never forsake Israel! He says it so many times that I can't even list them here!

How do the Arab Muslims get everyone to approve of them, no matter what horrible things they do? Oil! The Western countries are controlled by the multinational corporations under the Illuminati, the Council for Foreign Relations, and the Masons.

Scriptures always love Israel!

*They are Israelites, and to them belong the adoption, the glory, the covenants, the giving of the law, the worship, and the promises. To them belong the patriarchs, and from their race, according to the flesh, is the Christ who is God over all, blessed forever. Amen.*
ROMANS 9:4–5

*As the Scripture says, "Anyone who trusts in him will never be put to shame." For there is no difference between Jew and Gentile—the same Lord is Lord of all and richly blesses all who call on him, for, "Everyone who calls on the name of the Lord will be saved."*
ROMANS 10:11–13

*I do not want you to be ignorant of this mystery, brothers, so that you may not be conceited: Israel has experienced a hardening in part until the full number of the Gentiles has come in. And so all Israel will be saved, as it is written: "The deliverer will come from Zion; he will turn godlessness away from Jacob."*
ROMANS 11:25–26

Notice that the central core of the apostle Paul's argument regarding the Jewish people is: "For the gifts and calling of God are without repentance" (Romans 11:29 KJV). This means that once God makes a promise, He cannot and will not retract His word. God made a covenant promise in Genesis 15 that the seed of Abraham would inherit a certain portion of land. Add to this the testimony of the Christian martyr Stephen, as found in Acts 7:5, "[God] gave [Abraham] no inheritance here, not even a foot of ground. But God promised him that he and his descendants after him would possess the land, even though at that time Abraham had no child."

If, therefore, the land was promised to Abraham's seed; and if it has not yet been given to that seed; and if the gifts and calling of God are without repentance; then, of necessity, it follows that it will yet, at some future point in time, be given to the seed of Abraham, the people of Israel, for a possession.

## CAN THESE BONES LIVE?

The prophet Ezekiel was of a priestly family carried captive to Babylon in 597 B.C. His call to the prophetic ministry came as he dwelt among the captives who dwelt by the River Chebar at Tel Abib. One of the remarkable incidents he recorded was this:

> *The hand of the LORD was upon me, and he brought me*
> *out by the Spirit of the LORD and set me in the middle of a*
> *valley; it was full of bones. He led me back and forth among*
> *them, and I saw a great many bones on the floor of the valley,*
> *bones that were very dry. He asked me, "Son of man, can these*
> *bones live?" I said, "O Sovereign LORD, you alone know."*
> *Then he said to me, "Prophesy to these bones and say to*
> *them, 'Dry bones, hear the word of the LORD! This is what the*
> *Sovereign LORD says to these bones: I will make breath enter*
> *you, and you will come to life. I will attach tendons to you*
> *and make flesh come upon you and cover you with skin;*
> *I will put breath in you, and you will come to life.*
> *Then you will know that I am the LORD."'*
> EZEKIEL 37:1–6

Remarkably, we have witnessed the fullness of this miracle coming to pass. It has come about through a parade of conquerors who have taken over the land of Israel:

| | |
|---|---|
| 625 B.C. | Babylon |
| 536 B.C. | Medo-Persia |
| 270 B.C. | Ptolemais |
| 165 B.C. | Hasmoneans |
| 66 B.C. | Rome |
| A.D. 324 | Byzantium |
| 636 | Muslims |
| 1099 | Crusaders |
| 1187 | Saladin |
| 1229 | Franks |
| 1258 | Mamelukes |
| 1291 | Tartars |
| 1516 | Ottomans |
| 1878 | Britain |

For over a century the history of the Middle East has been moving in steady steps toward the fulfillment of this prophecy of Ezekiel.

- In 1878, after a ban of 1,743 years, Israelis were given permission to own property in the ancient land of their forefathers. They immediately established their first settlement, Petach Tikvah. Their return had begun.
- In 1897, Theodor Herzl issued a worldwide call to organize the Zionist movement.
- In 1917, Great Britain endorsed a Jewish state in the famous Balfour Declaration.
- From 1936–1945, over 6 million Jews were killed in the Nazi Holocaust.
- In 1948, as a result of a U.N. partition, Israel became a sovereign nation. Then, immediately challenged by an overpowering Arab force, an Israeli victory legitimized their declaration of statehood.

- In 1956, an invasion led by General Nasser of Egypt was soundly repelled.
- In 1967, the Six-Day War of Israel against another Arab coalition enlarged the borders of the new state and Jerusalem was united once again under Jewish control.
- In 1973, on the eve of the Jewish high holy day of Yom Kippur, a third Arab attack was again set back.
- In 1989, the dismantled countries of the Soviet Union permitted the Jewish refugees to return to Israel.
- In 1991 and 1992, repeated Scud attacks by Saddam Hussein of Iraq failed to dislodge the Israelis.

## THE COVENANT WITH ABRAHAM STANDS

In order to trace this covenant, we need to turn to the Genesis 12 account. There we find God approaching a man named Abram in the far-off city of Ur, in the land of the Chaldees. Abram is told to leave his land and journey to another, one which God would show him. There God would make a covenant, or pact, with him.

In obedience, Abram and his family trekked to the north and west, following the fertile crescent of the mighty Euphrates, to the city of Haran. This was where Abram's father, Terah, became ill and died. From thence it was that Abram and his entourage journeyed south, through the country of the Hittites into the land of Canaan.

It was there, close to Shechem, the modern Nablus on what the Arabs call the West Bank, that Abram first settled in the Promised Land. Further wanderings took him as far as Egypt and then back to Canaan: first to Bethel, north of Jerusalem, then finally to Mamre, in the vicinity of modern Hebron. It was there that God fulfilled His promise and made a covenant with him. The covenant is recorded for us in Genesis 15:7: "I am the LORD, who brought you out of Ur of the Chaldeans to give you this land to take possession of it."

Genesis 15:8–12 is a historical record of the various animal sacrifices Abram offered to ratify the covenant. Then, in verses 13–15,

Abram is informed that he would not personally inherit the land at that time. In verse 16, he is told that his descendants would be the ones to come into possession of the land in the fourth generation—in the time of Moses and Joshua. After sealing this covenant, in verse 17, God outlined the scope of the Promised Land in verses 18–21:

> *On that day the LORD made a covenant with Abram and said, "To your descendants I give this land, from the river of Egypt to the great river, the Euphrates—the land of the Kenites, Kenizzites, Kadmonites, Hittites, Perizzites, Rephaites, Amorites, Canaanites, Girgashites and Jebusites."*

Notice that the boundaries of the area promised to the descendants of Abram are defined in two distinctly different manners—first, by a geographical description; and second, by naming the inhabitants of the land at that time.

Let us note first the geographic description. Two specific borders are mentioned—the River of Egypt and the River Euphrates. Bible scholars are divided in their opinion as to the identity of the River of Egypt. Some say that it is the main trunk of the Nile. Others claim it to be the easternmost branch of the Nile near Suez. Still others argue for the Wadi el Arish, now a dry river bed in the eastern Sinai. I firmly believe that the term River of Egypt refers to the Wadi el Arish.

Ten enemy nations are listed to be dispossessed, while Joshua 3 catalogs only seven of them. The harmony between these two accounts is simple. The Genesis record covers all the tribes whose land Israel was to inherit, while the record in Joshua, written years later, omits the names of those nations that had already been conquered.

| Genesis 15:19–21 | Joshua 3:10 |
|---|---|
| Kenites | Hittites |
| Kenizzites | Perizzites |
| Kadmonites | Amorites |
| Hittites | Canaanites |
| Perizzites | Girgashites |

Rephaites      Jebusites

Amorites      Hivites

Canaanites

Girgashites

Jebusites

Let us locate these early peoples on a map of Palestine. We will deal first only with those who are listed in the Genesis account and note that they are either located in the Negev or east of the Jordan River, territory which Israel had already made secure before the text given in the book of Joshua.

The Kenites are mentioned first. They were ironworkers, living in the northern Sinai, near present-day Eilat. It was the Kenites who first mined copper at the spot known today as King Solomon's mines.

The Kenizzites were hunters who reputedly lived on the western slopes of Mount Seir, in the Wadi Arabah. This is due south of the Dead Sea, close to the famous red rock city of Petra.

The location of the Kadmonites is not definitely known. However, since their name means "easterners," it can be presumed that they lived east of the Jordan River. Tradition locates them at the foot of Mount Hermon in the Golan Heights.

The Rephaim were large men, giants as it were. According to Deuteronomy 3:11, they lived in Bashan, which lies east of the Jordan and south of the Sea of Galilee.

The next groupings are those names found in both the lists of Genesis and the book of Joshua. There are six tribes in this list, all located west of the Jordan River, from the Negev on the south through Lebanon on the north.

First, in this grouping, are the Hittites. There are two ancient people, both known as Hittites. One of these lived in the far north, in the present-day country of Turkey. These are the ancestors of the current Armenians. However, the Hittites referred to in the Genesis record are more probably the people known by archaeologists as the Hurrians. They dwelt in Lebanon, from the Mediterranean to the slopes of Mount Hermon.

The Perizzites are believed to have lived in the Shephelah, east of the Philistines of the Gaza Strip, but to the west of modern Hebron.

While the Genesis account locates the Amorites in the area of Gebron and Mamre, they are also found just north of the Arnon River in the Trans-Jordan. It was here that the Israelite troops, under the command of Moses, made the first approach to the Promised Land and engaged in battle with Sihon, king of Heshbon. Heshbon has been recently excavated by archaeologists and lies between Amman and Madaba in today's country of Jordan.

The Canaanites lived in the fertile farming area of the Plain of Sharon and the Valley of Jezreel. Their famous fortress city was Megiddo, whose location is undisputed today by archaeologists.

We are informed in Joshua 24:11 that the Girgashites dwelt west of Jordan, presumably in the Jordan valley itself, northward from Jericho to the city of Adam.

Finally, we come to the Jebusites, the early occupants of the city of Jerusalem. So strongly had they fortified this city, in fact, that it held out against the Israelites for nearly 500 years before being captured for David by his nephews Joab and Abishai.

There is one more tribe to consider, the Hivites, who, while not listed in the Genesis account, are named in the book of Joshua. They were probably omitted in Genesis because they were not recognized as a people in Abram's time but sprung up shortly thereafter. Two generations later, however, they evidently had come into existence and were located in the so-called West Bank area, at ancient Shechem, modern Nablus. It was a Hivite, a resident of this town, who defiled Dinah, the daughter of Jacob, in one of the uglier incidents in biblical history (Genesis 34).

———————————

In summary, we can see based on these descriptions that the true Israel is entitled to so much more property than has been allotted to them. We also know that the Lord will always intervene for the "apple of his eye" when she is in danger. And we know that those who bless

Israel will be blessed and those who curse Israel will be cursed.

Will the United States ever stop pressuring Israel to give up land for peace? I hope so, before it is to late. We must learn from our past mistakes and actions and realize that all these disasters that have come to America are not coincidence. I believe they are the acts of God in displeasure to His land being violated. The love-hate relationship must be reconciled between America and Israel, so that God once again can place His hand of blessing and protection on America, the land of the free and the home of the brave.

To contact Rabbi Michael Zeitler
for speaking at your church or
conference event, please call:

888-835-8093
Baruch Ha Shem

Messianic Ministries International
P.O. Box 333
Highland, NY 12528

To order additional copies of this book,
call Bronze Bow Publishing toll free at
866.724.8200
or go to
www.bronzebowpublishing.com

# ENDNOTES

[1] Pauline Moffitt Watts, "Science, Religion, and Columbus's Enterprise of the Indies," OAH *Magazine of History*, Vol. 5, No. 4 (Spring 1991): 14–17.

[2] Ibid.

[3] Ibid.

[4] B. Oren, "Jimmy Carter's Book: An Israeli View," *The Wall Street Journal*, December 26, 2006.

[5] A. F. Scott Pearson, *Church and State: Political Aspects of Sixteenth Century Puritanism* (Cambridge, England: Cambridge University Press, 1928), 11, 120, 123–24.

[6] Eugene Aubrey Stratton, *Plymouth Colony: Its History & People* (Salt Lake City, UT: Ancestry Pub., 1986), 17–18.

[7] Ibid., 18.

[8] Sacvan Bercovitch, *The Rites of Assent* (Albuquerque, NM: University of New Mexico Press, 1980), 12.

[9] George Washington, *A Collection of the Speeches of the President of the United States to Both Houses of Congress, at the Opening of Every Session, With Their Answers* (Boston: Manning and Loring, 1796).

[10] Manuel Noah, *Correspondence and documents relative to the attempt to negotiate for the release of the American captives at Algiers; including remarks on our relations with that Regency* (Washington City, 1816).

[11] Mitchell G. Bard, "Roots of the U.S.-Israel Relationship," Jewish Virtual Library website.

[12] Oren, "Jimmy Carter's Book: An Israeli View."

[13] Bard, "Roots of the U.S.-Israel Relationship."

[14] Ibid.

[15] Ibid.

[16] Herbert Hoover, "Hoover's Message to Jews Regarding 1929 Riots," Jewish Virtual Library website.

[17] Herbert Hoover, "Hoover's Message at the Organization Dinner of the American Palestine Committee, Washington, D.C., January 11, 1932," Jewish Virtual Library website.

[18] Philip Schaff and Henry Wace, *Nicene and Post-Nicene Fathers, Second Series, Vol. 14* (Buffalo, NY: Christian Literature Publishing Co., 1900).

[19] James Carroll, *Constantine's Sword* (New York: First Mariner Books, 2002), 178.

[20] Kathleen Tracy, *The Life and Times of Constantine* (Newark, DE: Mitchell Lane Publishers, 2005), 29.

[21] Hal Lindsey, "The 'Lawrence of Arabia' Legacy," *World Net Daily*, November 13, 2002.

[22] George Antonius, *The Arab Awakening* (London: Hamish Hamilton Publishers, 1938), 437–439.

[23] Meyer W. Weisgal, ed., *The Letters and Papers of Chaim Weizmann*, Series A, Volume VIII (Israel University Press, 1977), 197–206.

[24] Aharon Bregman and Jihan El-Tahri, *The Fifty Years War: Israel and the Arabs* (London: Penguin Books and BBC Books, 1998).

[25] Shlaim, *The Iron Wall: Israel and the Arab World* (New York: W. W. Norton and Company, 2001), 354–355.

[26] Burns, "We Should Talk to Our Enemies," *Newsweek*, October 25, 2008.

[27] Daniel Pipes, "Just Kidding: Syria's Peace Bluff," *The New Republic*, January 8–15, 1996: 18–19.

[28] Tomek Zadurowicz, *Israel and World Revivals* (Pasadena: Messiah's Harvest Ministries, 1997), 1–3.

[29] Ibid.

[30] Ibid.

[31] Shabtai Teveth, *Ben-Gurion and the Palestinian Arabs* (New York: Oxford University Press, 1985), 199–200.

[32] Mike Evans, *The Final Move Beyond Iraq* (Baltimore, MD: Frontline, 2007), 200.

33 Abraham Rabinovich, "Shattered Heights," *Jerusalem Post*, September 25, 1998.
34 Chris Mitchell, "God Protect Us in Battle," The Christian Broadcasting Network, October 16, 2005.
35 Roslyn Bailey, "Miracles During the First Gulf War," a tract from Jerusalem, October 1999.
36 *Yated Ne`eman*, February 2, 1991.
37 Ibid.
38 Ibid.
39 Bailey, "Miracles During the First Gulf War."
40 *Yated Ne`eman*, February 22, 1991.
41 Samuel, *Missiles, Masks, and Miracles* (Jerusalem: Executive Learning Center of Aish HaTorah, 1991).
42 *Yated Ne`eman*, January 25, 1991.
43 Bailey, "Miracles During the First Gulf War."
44 Ibid.
45 Ibid.
46 Ibid.
47 Ibid.
48 Ibid.
49 Samuel, *Missiles, Masks, and Miracles*.
50 "Classroom Hit With Students Waiting Outside," *Arutz Sheva National News*, May 21, 2006.
51 Jeremy Last, "Breslavers See Miracle in Rocket Miss," *The Jerusalem Post*, July 23, 2006: 3.
52 Ibid.
53 Jenny Hazan, "Chabad Synagogue Heavily Damaged in Nahariya: Torah Scrolls Safe and Sound After Rocket Attack," Chabad-Lubavitch Media Center, July 20, 2006.
54 Steve Quayle, "Iran's Military Exercise and Apocalyptic Plans for Israel and World, http://www.stevequayle.com/News.alert/06_Unrest/060821.Iran.apocal.html.
55 Pierce De Lacy Henry Johnstone, *Muhammad and His Power* (New York: C. Scribner's Sons, 1901), 127.
56 "The Balfour Declaration," Jewish Virtual Library website.
57 Antonius, *The Arab Awakening*, 437–439.
58 "Framework for Peace in the Middle East, Agreed at Camp David," Jewish Virtual Library website.
59 "Peace Treaty Between Israel and Egypt," Jewish Virtual Library website.
60 Mitchell Bard, "The Lebanon War," Jewish Virtual Library website.
61 Avi Shlaim, *Israel and Palestine: Reappraisals, Revisions, Refutations* (Brooklyn, NY: Verso, 2009).
62 Ibid.
63 Ibid.
64 "Agreement on the Gaza Strip and the Jericho Area," Jewish Virtual Library website.
65 "The Oslo II Agreement," Jewish Virtual Library website.
66 Ibid.
67 "The Wye Plantation," Jewish Virtual Library website.
68 Glenn Kessler, "Talking Points Aside, Bush Stance on Palestinian State Is Not a First," *Washington Post*, October 5, 2005.
69 Yediot Yeshurun newsletter, June 2001.
70 Wolf Blitzer, *Territory of Lies* (New York: Harper & Row, 1989), 219–224.
71 Amir Oren, "The Right to Strike," *Haaretz*, April 23, 2007.